FISHERMAN'S VALLEY

FISHERMAN'S VALLEY

SEASONAL TIPS
FOR COARSE ANGLERS

John Bailey

David & Charles

Photographs by the author and his great friends
Martin H. Smith, Johnny Jensen and Jim Tyree

A DAVID & CHARLES BOOK

A catalogue record for this book is available from the British
Library.

ISBN 0-7153-9934-9

Book designed by Michael Head
Typeset by Ace Filmsetting Ltd, Frome, Somerset,
and printed in Italy by Milanostampo SpA
for David & Charles
Brunel House   Newton Abbot   Devon

CONTENTS

INTRODUCTION

The Valley

This story of a season on my most cherished waters is rooted in over thirty years of knowledge and love. I hope you will excuse me if I have changed their names to some extent in order to protect them. The map, too, is only vaguely accurate, if such a thing is possible! Again I have taken geographical liberties to guard against invasion and indeed to avoid the rage of the owners of private pools. I hope you do not think that these peripheral deceptions are important for, after all, what mature angler wants to steal another's waters? And the central purpose of the book is totally sincere: by recording my observations on the waters of the valley I hope to teach a little about the behaviour of fish through the seasons and suggest some ways to outwit the largest and craftiest of them. The book is not a chain of success stories because no real fishing life is like that and, if it were, it would soon become monotonous and meaningless. Nor do I think that success can be measured simply by a big fish on the bank: the ability to watch a fish and learn from it *in the water* is a triumph in itself. The skills involved in fish watching and in understanding the water are just as great as in fish catching and can be infinitely more rewarding.

What about the waters of the valley themselves? In simple terms, the ice sheets of the Great Ice Age that lasted for several hundreds of thousands of years moved in and out of the region at least three times. These spreads of ice deposited large amounts of sand, gravels and clays that have since weathered in many places into large areas of fertile soil. And such was the immensity and power of the ice that it dumped rocks and minerals in both huge ridges and gently undulating layers. So it was this great, cold hand that sculptured the lush rolling landscape of the valley today.

The melting ice created a massive river and it also swamped the rock strata beneath so that springs would bubble up for centuries afterwards. Initially, this river was vast, far larger than the Thames or the Trent today. It was unruly and forged its way north and westwards and probably emptied into a massive estuary along with the river Rhine itself. Gradually however, over thousands of years, it shrank back between more restrictive banks and by Roman times it was narrow enough to be dammed and for mills to be created to control its shrunken proportions even further.

From its beginning, the floor of the valley always possessed standing water in the form of swamps and oxbow lakes, but again it was the Romans who built the first fish ponds. Between 1100 and 1530 the monks added to these and it is possible that some of the waters today are founded upon ancient stewponds that would provide carp, fresh for Friday's religious observances.

However, it was the eighteenth century that really witnessed the emergence of the valley as it appears today. This was the period of the Agricultural Revolution when the great estates were constructed on the profits from sheep

SEA

Estuary

Marshes

Road to Wood Pigeons

TIDAL RIVER

Stream

Gardeners Lake

Frog Hall

Wood

Old Trout Lake

Hall Lake

Stream

Stream

Lily Lake

Road to Moonstone

Track

The Crucian Puddle

Road to the Wildfowl Pit

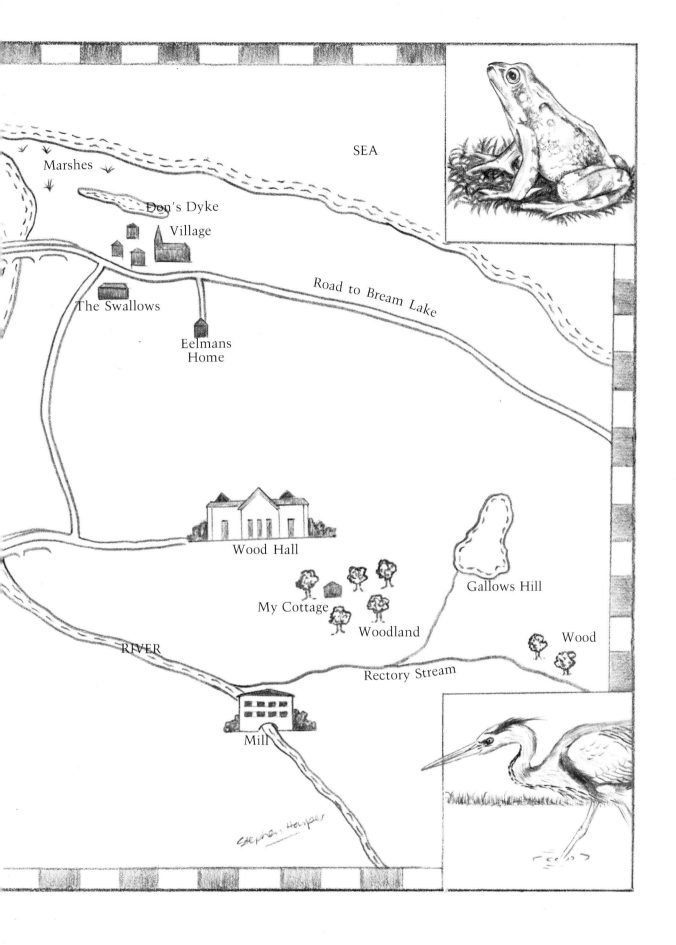

SEA

Marshes

Don's Dyke

Village

The Swallows

Eelmans
Home

Road to Bream Lake

Wood Hall

My Cottage

Woodland

Gallows Hill

Wood

RIVER

Rectory Stream

Mill

and increased crop productivity. Between 1740 and 1780 four halls and eight more lakes were created. Furthermore marl, a natural mixture of lime and clay, had been dug from many pits to be spread on the fields as a fertiliser: the holes produced filled with the winter rains so the whole valley sparkled with water. At this time the extensive woodlands were planted, too: in the gracious eighteenth century it was considered that no landed estate was complete without either water or woodland, and many of the oaks were planted and the lakes dug during the same decades many years ago.

All these waters became stocked both naturally and artificially. Whenever the river flooded, some of the lowest-lying pools became colonised by roach, dace, perch, pike and eels. The carp that the monks had introduced from the continent tended to live on either in their old-established waters, or they were taken out and stocked into new ones. Tench were also introduced by man as a valuable food and sporting resource; and eels made their way everywhere, flooding into the water course as tiny elvers in the springtime and staying on for decades to grow fat. Bream and rudd were frequently brought by horse and cart from the broads, not *too* far away to the south and east so transportation was a feasible operation. Of course the fish populations have changed dramatically over the centuries and nothing beneath the surface of any of the waters is entirely stable. For example, the native wild carp the monks ate have now become extremely rare, even in the valley. Here, as everwhere, they have been replaced to a large extent by the larger and more voracious mirror carp imported from southern Europe. Rudd, too, appear to be on the decline, and roach populations in a river are never constant. Perch peak and then decline again, and even large pike seem to flare up for only a few years out of many. Indeed, over the thirty years that I have known the valley, I myself have seen sometimes subtle and sometimes dramatic changes take place in the fish populations.

Even when agriculture hiccoughed in the 1870s the newly risen commercial and industrial rich had discovered the charms of the valley and built great houses of their own, with at least three more of the by then obligatory lakes. In fact, by the turn of this century, not only did the valley possess its river and associated streams, but also nearly a score of lakes, pools and ponds and a similar number of small field pits. The last major influence on its structure began in World War II. Airfields were required in great number, and gravel and sand were dug from many pits along the river valley, a process continued today by the demand for more roads, bypasses and industrial and domestic estates. In short, when I arrived in the late 1950s this was a boy angler's wonderland that agricultural and industrial development, in its infancy, had not even begun to affect. Everything in it seemed more vital, and the fish were undoubtedly bigger than any I had seen before; even after thirty years I still feel its special spell. No matter how fabulous it is to fish away in Asia or in Europe, it is marvellous to come home.

The variety of the fish and the waters they live in is never-ending, and for

A typical splash of water in the valley. During a summer rainstorm a spring has bubbled up and overflowed through the foliage and it will sweep a mass of food forms into the lake at Gallows Hill

me it became something of a passion to watch how the differing seasons
affected this world of water. I soon realised that there are continuing influences
at work on the water, on its vegetation, on its birds, mammals, fish, insects,
amphibians and even molluscs. I took to watching the ponds, pools and river
in all seasons, from high summer to bleak midwinter, fascinated by the changes
wrought by the different months. My aim has always been to put every piece
together and fit them into a giant jigsaw of the natural world.

There have always been friends in these explorations, although obsession
exhausted most of them and they flagged, eventually to watch with interest
and encouragement from the sidelines. Also off and on over the years there has
been Don (this is not his real name; I have changed this too, to protect him
like the waters themselves) who happened to appear during an important
period with an eagerness that temporarily matched or even surpassed my
own—and that in itself is worth recording.

SEASONAL CHANGES

Winter

In no other season does the weather vacillate more wildly and have such a dramatic effect on the waterside and water temperatures. Gradually the water loses its warmth, reaching its coldest point around January and even into February, although this depends very much on the weather. The trees have lost their leaves, the reeds are dead, and waterweeds have rotted apart from those grouped around the springs in the stillwaters or such warmer water influences in rivers as inflowing streams. Many, if not most water insects have died off or are hibernating, so that food and shelter are both considerably reduced; in fact waters often clear out after the first frost as the cold will soon kill all algae growths. As a result, fish are less and less likely to shift from what cover they can find. They feel vulnerable in the clear water, and there is little incentive to travel in search of food. All this is part of the natural cycle, for as the temperatures decrease so the metabolism of fish slows, and as they need less and less food so the urge to move declines accordingly.

Fish can be all but static according to their species and to the weather. Carp will frequently hold up for periods of days or weeks at a time under fallen trees or in the remains of weed or lilybeds. At this time they are virtually comatose and can be lifted out on an oar, only sliding off at the last minute to waddle drunkenly away. Tench sink into depressions in the bottom, half in the silt and leaf fall; here they are prone to be foul-hooked by a pike spinner worked slow and deep. It is quite common for parasites to be found on them, now able to secure a good hold on the recumbent fish. The perch shoals will work around any underwater snag until the falling light encourages them out to feed. The smaller fish lie in deeper areas of open water, generally well clear of reedbeds, islands or any other predatorial ambush point. Again these small fish wait for the light to drop on mild days, lending a degree of security when they roam for food should they occasionally feel the need.

All this behaviour is intensified as the weather becomes colder. As depressions are replaced by anticyclones, the skies clear, winds develop teeth, daytime temperatures drop from 46°F to 28° or 26°F, and overnight frosts often become intense under clear moons. The stillwaters freeze and even the rivers carry ice down the margins, or perhaps all across on the slower, ponded stretches. Life goes on during these periods but even more intermittently. Pike, especially, can be seen under the ice on a steady prowl during their usual feeding periods. For those anglers hardy enough, they can be caught through holes chipped Eskimo-fashion through the ice. But, of course, the sheet must be thick enough for safety and must not be trusted once any thaw has started. Indeed this is not something I would really do myself, or encourage—I only use the information gleaned from the work of a few men to make the point that we do know pike still move and feed in a comparatively normal fashion.

Carp may occasionally be seen blowing mud up under the ice, especially if a spring or a stream brings in a little warmth. Sometimes the ice freezes gin-clear and it is possible to watch shoals of small roach moving slowly, cautiously, pecking at bits of food. All movements though, are very slow in a silent, cold, often dark world.

On the rivers, the current demands a little more movement from the fish: chub, dace or grayling, for example, inhabiters of the faster water, are almost constantly active through the very severest weather. Roach and bream will still exhibit signs of life and will feed in even the most savage periods, very often long after dark. No matter how quickly the temperatures plummet, the period between 6pm and midnight will see some sort of feeding activity take place, albeit in a slow, unhurried fashion. The water temperature is by now relatively stable and the fish are waiting for the security of maximum darkness. For this reason, the nights of a new moon see the earliest and the most activity. Inexplicable—to me anyway—are the occasional daytime feeding spells that both roach and bream enjoy which, contrary to all their normal rules, are frequently between 11am and 2pm in periods of maximum light. Once, on a day of temperatures hovering around freezing point, a shoal of roach began to move on the surface for several minutes and two or three fish came quickly to the net. I have heard it suggested that a morning sunlight does something to lift the temperatures and give the fish some encouragement; however, the thermometer does not confirm this theory, and in all probability it is another example of one of Nature's unfathomable secrets.

1947, 1963, 1981: these were the winters when a cold snap developed into virtually arctic conditions. In such a period anticyclones hang over the country it seems interminably, channelling in winds from the north and east. The weather becomes Siberian, and for weeks temperatures never even approach zero: the rivers freeze bank to bank, and the shallower stillwaters become almost solid. Some of the species now sink into the silt, which will retain its moisture even when the water is frozen; carp and tench may be visible only by their backs and a ridge of dorsal fin. Under normal circumstances they will come to little or no harm, unless the conditions persist and the silt itself begins to solidify, when the last of the oxygen resources will be used up. For example, when shallow stillwaters unfroze in the spring of 1963, terrible carnage was witnessed in many places. Bream shoals suffered particularly and whole populations were virtually wiped out. Roach were similarly decimated, and in some areas even the generally indomitable tench and carp were found destroyed. Wild carp—the original English species, slim of body and tough as leather—were the only ones to appear virtually indestructible. It seems almost as though they can be deep frozen and still come through unscathed.

These periods are rare, and our more usual weather consists of depressions tracking in from the Atlantic, bringing grey skies, rain and temperatures which are generally quite mild. Ice melts as the low pressure covers the country, and water temperatures rise and hold steady as night cloud-cover keeps the warmth in—it rarely allows a frost. Rain also induces activity in the fish: it introduces oxygen that stimulates the entire system, and if it is hard enough, it brings a taint of colour into previously gin-clear water—even if visibility is clouded just a little, fish feel much more confident to move and feed. Also, the amount of food that is swept in by the heavier rainstorms is considerable. Earthworms, for example, make up a significant part of a river fish's larder when the rains really come. A recent survey suggested that up to ten thousand lobworms could be washed into a one-mile stretch of a major river system during a twenty-four-hour period. That represents a very great deal of food for the thousand or so decent fish resident there.

Then it rains . . . and rains . . . and rains. The river rises, colours, rises still. It runs bank high. Now it is over the banks . . . over the fields . . . and is a flood, drowning bridges, roads and even villages. The larger the river, the wider the area it will deluge, but even small watercourses can flood a dramatic portion of the valley floor. Many fish simply stick to their hideouts and the river floods way above their heads, as they lie buried deep into willow roots or hidden in the calm of an undercut.

When the full force of the water falls back a little and the all-important barometer begins to rise, then some fish, chub especially, will begin to roam. An ingrained sense tells them that the time is ripe for pickings, and they follow the water through field after field over flooded farmland, gorging on dislodged spiders, flies, ants, beetles and worms as they travel. Generally the fish sense the water thinning out around them and drop back into the river intact and in time. Sometimes, though, they are stranded in ditches or field depressions, prey to herons, cats and foxes. Occasionally they find a new home altogether: as the water recedes, it leaves them in a low-lying stillwater and the marooned chub or roach learn to live in a new, restricted environment—often with surprising results. The chub that finds the small, overstocked roach pond and thrives to 6lb or over; the roach that find the deep, clear, rich sandpit and add 8oz to their weight in their first year there. Even gudgeon are inveterate travellers and occasionally find secluded waters that allow them to break the ¼lb barrier and measure a mighty eight inches!

Another major feature of the winter weather patterns is a series of high winds. These can be quite as strong as the equinoctial gales of late October and have mixed blessings on the waterside. The trees are purged of their dead timber but birds can be killed, blown from their night roosts and, in the case of geese and swans, thrown off course into power lines. Indeed fishing in woodland can be dangerous; and never do as one of my friends once did . . . tied his basket to his umbrella! A big wind can be beneficial in several ways: firstly, a gale is almost always from the west and will bring in comparatively mild, cloudy conditions. Secondly, vitally, the constant battery of a water by wind has strange effects: eventually even a small lake begins to rock quite noticeably. Steady currents build up and they gradually start to energise many fish species and shake them into a positive feeding mode. On large waters the drifts and undertows can be quite as powerful as any river current in places. These underwater flows are not constant throughout the water but when they can be found, by casting out empty swim feeders and monitoring their progress, roach and bream will certainly be located there. I am almost sure that these currents stir the bottom to a certain extent, creating slightly cloudy water streams and pushing dislodged food along with them. Further, the increased activity of prey fish triggers predators into an aggressive mood and a large wind will see some of the best pike fishing of the winter.

Obviously, the approach of a gale causes the barometer to fall—generally the kiss of death to waterside activity and, certainly, the best of all sport seems to be after the wind has blown for some hours, is actually moderating a little and the glass is at least steadying if not on the upturn. Three favourable things are then combined: the water is warmed and oxygenated, the currents have been activated and the air pressure is rising.

And then it can snow. In a few hours I have seen the wind-driven snow heap in drifts ten to twelve feet high on the river plain, isolating the barns, filling the frozen dykes and forming great banks against the hedgerows and mills. To be caught on the floodplain by a heavy snowstorm is a terrible experience and much like being overtaken by a dense fog. Even at midday it soon becomes impossible to make out familiar objects which generally serve as landmarks. Trees, mills, cattlesheds and barns are obscured by the fast-falling flakes and the quickly rising drifts. The footpaths across the marsh are soon obliterated and often I have only reached home by following the direction of the wind. In the snow the footprints of birds, stoats and weasels make varied patterns and you can trace them for long distances across the flats and the banks. Otters often leave behind them the spoor by which you can easily follow them to their nests or lairs. How they live during the really bitter weeks when the ice is two feet thick is hard to say. Perhaps the coots and the waterhens provide what the frozen lakes and rivers deny.

Stillwaters lie covered in ice and coated in snow, barely distinguishable from the land around. In the water this is the deadest time of all, as everything beneath the ice mantle is starved of oxygen, warmth and light. We can only guess at the half-life in these gloomy days; possibly most fish feed sporadically, drifting through the haziness for a while, though overwintering insects are deep in the bed, under stones or buried in the roots of weeds. Only around warm springs is there still any sign of activity. Actually, one year at Lily Lake a band of watercress lived a cold winter out, like green lips around the life-giving water which gushed in from a spring at around 50°F.

The river runs like a black wound through the whiteness, and though the intense cold has its dire effects, fishing is possible and some attempt at underwater guesswork can be made. It is the same old story: activity has slowed to a snail's pace and what fish move will wait till complete darkness—with very odd exceptions that is, almost too infrequent to mention; for example once I saw a very big roach in the river rising for crusts at 3pm in the midst of a snowstorm. Explain that if you can! Ultimately, when examining Nature, we only know the depths of our own ignorance.

Winters are critical. If a warm settled summer is followed by a mild damp winter, then the fry drive has a hope of pushing through to its second year. Extreme cold cuts through their numbers: long spells of snow starve them: heavy rain is also bad for survival rates on the river. Simply, the river today is not that of a half-century ago. Dredging is more ruthless and so excess water is carried faster and with greater force to the sea, especially so now that the old cornmills are private dwellings. Incomers understand river dynamics only a little and are afraid of them. Sluice gates are flung open and remain wide from the first flood. The water roars through and, denied of cover upriver, a great many of the unfortunate fingerlings cannot resist the current and are swept downstream, in all probability to their deaths.

Still, every winter has to end, hard or not, and the wheel of the year will inevitably turn towards spring and new hope . . .

— *Spring* —

Spring rarely settles in as a season of gradually swelling warmth. False dawns are frequent, sometimes coming as early as February when the sun shines, the wind drops and flies appear on the cracks in the masonry. Such a day will see a cold night following it however, and any temperature rise is quickly nullified. Water temperatures only really begin to mount steadily and without interruption in the latter part of March—yet even in April there may be sleet, fogs and rainstorms which can bring checks and reverses.

As the water warms, however, subtle changes take place; to start with, fresh weed begins to push through the detritus of the bed, and all this rubbish and dead material rises as a rotting scum to the surface some time in April. The river becomes clogged with the stuff, and where it gathers on the windward shores of stillwaters it can begin to smell noticeably. There is every evidence to suggest that fish do not enjoy this period of the 'lifting', and certainly the trout fishing is quiet at such times. However, the process does not last long and soon the water clears and fresh weed becomes evident.

Inevitably, it is in this dynamic period that the coarse fish begin to spawn. Pike are generally the first to make their moves in late February, continuing through March and occasionally into April. Like all species, they seek out traditional sites: the shallow reeded bays of the large pits or lakes; areas of rotted stumps, dead lilies or fallen masonry; or frequently the mouths of feeder streams that lead into the river. The females, generally the biggest fish in the water, assemble early, arriving singly or in small groups. The jacks, the smaller males, gather together in the vicinity moving in and out of the nerve centre as the spawning commences. It is quite amazing how larger pike will live and spawn in a quite tiny feeder stream—sometimes it is hard to see how they can even turn around. Yet even though the water barely covers them, they remain well hidden, such is the perfection of their camouflage. After spawning, many of the pike do not leave their redds at once; certainly those that spawn in the feeder stream do not. Perhaps Nature intends them to linger on to give their eggs some protection from the eels and roach that would otherwise move in. Perhaps she also offers them a 'bribes day', when the frogs and toads emerge from the meadows to spawn in the very same feeder streams. It is obvious to all of us that these creatures attract the herons, but unseen to us, many disappear down the maws of the ever more hungry pike.

Then there is a pause until some time later in May when the roach and bream congregate in their turn, again on newly emerged weedbeds that are used year after year, generation after generation. The spawning itself occupies between two and four days, providing the critical water temperature remains constant. Should a cold easterly blow or heavy rain fall, then there will be a pause until the spawning beds reheat.

This is when the eels move in to gorge on the eggs, often feeding within inches of the discharging females. At the peak of the bream spawning period, possibly 90 or even 95 per cent of the water's eel population will be concentrated. Happily there are eggs enough for the eels and for the future: a large female bream can lay three hundred thousand eggs.

Pike, long since spawned and now feeding heavily, also drift towards the action; tired fish, wounded fish and sexually pre-occupied fish are all potential targets. Very large pike will move long distances at this time, steadily and with a distinct purpose. For example, the dace of the river always congregate in late May on the gravel beds below the mill, and shadowing them will be the forms of the largest pike in the whole beat. It is no fluke that the pike are there—as the dace spawn, this is their position, every year; it is part of pike lore, and is passed on somehow from generation to generation.

Predatory fish are not the only creatures to profit at the expense of the spawning bream and roach. Grebes circle the area and herons stalk the reedbed waiting for the weary or exhausted straggler. Even the gulls will move in from the coast, knowing there will be small roach in plenty near the water's surface, knowing that out of birth comes death and food.

Down on the river the school of barbel chooses the same area as the dace to spawn, just a little downstream where the water runs deeply but still quickly over gravel and newly emerged ranunculus weed. It is easy to watch the fish through Polaroid glasses, flashing, rolling and even leaping clear of the water. They never look more beautiful than at this time, in their own ponderous way, their colours exceptionally vivid and their bodies particularly dark red, fins flashing in the blur and golden stomachs gleaming like sword-thrusts. After spawning the barbel move away a little and begin to clean themselves, just as Patrick Chalmers recorded the Thames barbel behaving long ago:

> The bright shadows were the spawned barbel, rolling like cats rolled sidelong in the sun, clean themselves and preen themselves at the tail of the weir.

Tench, I suspect, live the year out on the edge of dreams, in that blissful state of waking sleepiness that comes to us all in the half-consciousness after the alarm clock rings. Should the weather become extraordinarily mild then they might stir, wander about and even feed a little. If there is a very heavy warm rain, so that the water rises and colours, they might be flushed out for a little while to feed, but in half-hearted fashion.

In spring however, when the temperature rises, the days stretch out and the light becomes more intense, the tench shake themselves and begin to stir properly, their new year in mind. Spawning, though, is still a very long way off in most years—only exceptionally high temperatures will see them active before June. Through late May though, they are often preparing, the males tending to gather into gangs whilst the females travel singly or in small groups. Often a female will be chased by four or five smaller males eager for foreplay. Day by day the females become more distended by the bulk of their eggs, and if temperatures never rise high enough for the tench to release them, by July they can look like footballs with fins. More frequently, though, brief spells of spawning commence around the start of June, often taking place towards the end of a sunny day when the water is at its warmest. Not all the tench necessarily take part, and those that do are sometimes half-hearted about the business. Still, eggs are shed and fertilised, and not all the eels are attracted to the feast as they will be when the final, full-blown revelries take place.

Tench are predominantly margin spawners. Activity rarely takes place far out from the bank and the normal release of eggs is against reeds and bulrushes, preferably over a relatively hard, clean, stony bottom. Soft reed and lilies are also used, but are not as important for tench as they are for carp.

When the carp spawn the whole lake knows about it. At its peak, a huge gyrating body of fish will churn up yards of water, spawning orgiastically against reeds, weeds, lilies, roots, draping branches, masonry—almost anything that their blind progress takes them to. It is hardly surprising that the spawning of the carp is so violent or so protracted: a 20lb carp can contain between one and two million eggs. Early- to mid-spring temperatures only sometimes rise high enough to induce spawning: from June onwards is the most likely period and even into August as the water warms towards the ideal of around 70°F.

Spring can be a time of immense danger, especially for bream. Let me explain . . . It was a cold spring. Water temperatures looked like climbing in late April, but a May of constant cold easterlies, fogs and occasionally sleet-cold rain never allowed them above the low to mid-fifties Fahrenheit. June saw no great improvement and the only major difference was the entire absence of rain.

A vast shoal of large, old bream became increasingly ripe with eggs and milt but, however great their trauma, the water remained several degrees too cold for them to begin release. Not until early in July was there a change, and then it was cataclysmic. The world rocketed from spring to high summer in twenty-four hours: the sun beat down; the nights were milky warm; the water temperatures soared and within four days of the heatwave starting, the big bronze fish were spawning hard and desperately.

Within seventy-two hours they had finished. They were exhausted—but the sun continued to blaze and water temperatures to rise. There had been no rain for six weeks and oxygen levels fell very low, lethally so for aged, stressed fish. A big male—easily identified by the white spawning tubercles on his head and gill flaps—was the first to die just before dawn when the oxygen was at its lowest. The body floated into the reeds and the parasites began to swarm on it, after a heron had taken an eye out and rats had gnawed at the tail root. Soon the sun shone on the corpse, the milky water continued to heat well over the 70°F mark, and the carcass started to bloat and to rot. That very process used up further oxygen, and as the sun continued to shine, more water evaporated and one by one, further bream drifted to the surface, gasping on their sides. Most lingered into the night before dying under the stars.

By the end, a hundred and forty bream were gone, all weighing between 8 and 14lb. Most rotted down to remain in the bowels of their lake; others were dragged out and buried in the adjacent woodland, and a single one was sound enough to be set up by a local taxidermist . . . a permanent reminder of what havoc a cold spring can wreak.

As the water warms through April and May and as the marsh plants and waterweeds grow, the insects resume their lives in their millions up and down the valley watercourses. For years I was unaware of them. However, I could not see them because Nature intended that I should not. If I, untrained, could see these insects, so could the birds, and then the insects would be easily destroyed and the plants which they keep in check would choke the lakes, pools and river in a couple of seasons.

After thirty years, I am only just penetrating some of the disguises that keep so many different water insects safe from their feathered enemies. For example, there are some that live on the great water dock which are plant-like green and live out their entire lives on the leaf, never venturing off their vegetable world. Other red-coloured ones live solely amongst the flowers of purple loosestrife, whilst yellow ones inhabit honeysuckle, and black ones cling to the dark glutinous mud of the pond. Some big water beetles effectively resemble inedible acorns, others mimic the droppings of the birds of the reed margins; and the insects that live on reeds themselves are long and thin, whilst those that inhabit lilypads are squat and round and look like seeds.

Whenever fish and their habits are under discussion, reference will inevitably be made to water reeds and weeds; these are the essential buildings in the aquatic world, and as the water warms up through the spring all manner of plants develop and serve vital functions. It is well known that green plants are instrumental in breaking up carbon dioxide: in those which are aquatic the released oxygen is retained by the water in a dissolved state, and is therefore available to fish, beetles, shrimps, nymphs and all the host of living organisms.

Secondly, waterweeds consolidate the bed of the river and knit together the gravels and small stones in times of flood. If these were swept away, larvae and stone-living creatures would be destroyed and fish food levels would suffer.

Thirdly, weed provides cover for small fish in their early, vulnerable stages of life when every predator is out to seize them. It also gives shelter to all fish from the full force of the currents of both still- and running water, and also from the glare of the sun. Without weed all fish become nervy, neurotic creatures, like we would be ourselves in a world devoid of vegetation.

Fourthly, weed provides ambush cover from which pike and perch can launch their attacks on prey; and fifth and finally, waterweeds of all sorts provide homes and breeding places for the innumerable algal forms and tiny organisms that are the basis of the entire food chain. Whilst we curse weed and watch its growth through May with alarm, it is as well to consider what deserts our waters would be without them, and to praise the spring for its many bounteous gifts.

Summer

The footpaths along the river and around the stillwaters are nearly hidden by tall, drooping grasses. Many of the dykes and ditches are almost completely choked up with hemlocks, frogbits and marshwort, so that open water spaces are few and far between. Innumerable butterflies—amongst them handsome black and yellow swallowtails and gorgeous red admirals—are fluttering over the meadows and along the rose-decked hedgerows. Here and there the marshes are pink with orchids and flecked with a white spray of wild parsley that attracts little moths poised on almost invisibly beating wings. This is the season of the bellflowered buckbean, the marsh thistle and the bog pimpernel. The whole valley is now a great wildflower garden: marsh, dyke, riverside, aldercarr and even the swampy margins of the pool all have their brilliant blossoms, and the summer breeze is laden with their aroma.

The swallows are busy hunting midges over the marsh, for they have young to feed in nests under the doorways of boathouses and in the upper storeys of the mill. The swifts, too, continually circle the rivers and pool, but sometimes rising so high in the air as to become almost invisible. The air is full of the sound of rooks, of wood pigeons and pheasants, and as dusk approaches, the sound of an owl. Evening sets in, and the fragrance of the waterside wildflowers becomes stronger than it was during the daytime. Thousands of moths begin fluttering over the river, the pond and the stillwaters. In a copse near the river a nightjar begins churring—a weird, mysterious, haunting voice of the night. It appears like a shadow in the gloom of the copse and flies now silently, now with flapping wings, around the margin of the watermeadow.

This is a vision of the ideal, and a good summer is critical. If the weather is warm and stable then the food organisms multiply; continuing good weather sees the spread of microscopic algae throughout the stillwaters and in the slower areas of the river. It is upon this minute food source that the countless multitude of water-fleas depends. These spread through the water system like Milky Ways made up of countless millions of edible items; in times of plenty there can be so many of these tiny creatures that they colour whole bands of the water a rusty red or a bluey green. The water-flea is a fascinating creature; it moves in jerks brought about by the use of its branched antennae, and thus goes about its business, eating items of algae. The water-fleas themselves are heavily predated upon by pond-skaters, water-boatmen and swan-mussels, all of which filter the water and extract the water-fleas for food.

Whole belts of water become soupy with food, and this season of plenty benefits fish from fifty years to fifty days of age. The mature carp, tench, bream, roach and rudd will sup in the clouds of water-fleas hour upon hour, expending only the slightest effort to grow fat. Though this can be an exasperating time for the angler when any bait larger than the sliver of a pinhead will be ignored, he must realise that this is a vital period in the lives of the big fish he venerates.

More essentially, the abundance of this food 'dust' is the key to the future of the waters: the fry of the spring are assured full little bellies and, therefore, life itself. Their first few weeks in the world are critical and must be survived, and a prolific larder is essential. Equally obviously, the quicker and stronger the tiny fish grow, the better chance there is of them meeting the harsher conditions of autumn and winter with some hope. It is all a question of percentages: of how many eggs will survive the predation of eels, other fish, their very parents, beetles, bugs and water birds; of how many will hatch out free of disease; of how many will prosper through the summer, and of how many will be alive to see their second year. A favourable spring, a bountiful summer and a benign winter will tip the scales of life and can produce a year

One of the beautiful and well-established field pits. Though small, these waters can be very rich and provide surprisingly large fish

class of sufficient quality and quantity to resurrect a declining fishery. The effects are seen everywhere: the more fry grow through to fingerlings, the more food is available to small perch and pike. A shoal of 4oz perch in particular is as voracious as a pack of piranhas, and will consume tens of thousands of tiny fish through a long summer. Such a period is vital in pushing these perch to 8–12oz, a size large enough to take gudgeon and 3in fish. In turn, such a diet will catapult them to 1½ or 2lb, a size large enough to permit them to tackle any fish up to 5oz in weight.

A generous summer does not benefit fish alone. The grebes will see their entire family survive, and the kingfishers will continue to build up after the last disastrous winter when their numbers were cut nearly to nothing. And though the growing fry are too small for otters or their cubs, the promise that they represent could attract the animals to the water in the future.

The summer should be a joyful time in any water system. The willows and alders look at their best, the yellow flag and the reedbeds positively glow, the

(opposite) *A typical view out over one of the estates in the valley. In the foreground is the elaborate walled garden where the Hall's vegetables and fruit are grown. Beyond is the parkland, and beyond that the manmade lake glints in the distance*

lilies blossom and the waterweed drifts in whole fields of deep fertile green. Water temperatures that are stable in the upper sixties or low seventies encourage a wonderful world of insects. All manner of flies and nymphs, of beetles, aquatic spiders, snails and of dragonflies are at their most active over the milky warm water.

This is the time that fish—and carp especially—manage to look almost humanly happy. Never tell a carp fisher that his quarry does not relish sunbathing—stretching his dorsal fin, pectorals beating warm water down his flanks, his eyes roll in something near to a carp sleep. Tench, too, hanging in the shade of a lilybed, look something like a Mexican under a sombrero. Rudd glitter like sovereigns and barbel glow like golden cats. . . These warm days between late June and late August are quite obviously those of ease and plenty and maximum enjoyment in the fish's world. Even the eel rippling luxuriously in the warm blanket weed must come close to something like pleasure, and realise that the way it is behaving is something other than a survival instinct.

Watching how fish behave in warm, clear water, armed with Polaroids, binoculars, stealth and patience, must be as rewarding an exercise as there is. Often fishing in such conditions is just about futile, as once air temperatures climb into the eighties and stay there most fish become more and more reluctant to feed, on large food items especially. These periods generally involve cool clear nights, which themselves rarely see a great deal of feeding activity. The first hour of darkness and a short period around dawn are possibly the most reliable feeding times for most fish, though there are exceptions. For example, however hot it becomes, carp will browse now and again in the surface film, and barbel will flash on well oxygenated gravels for small baits like hemp if introduced in sufficient quantity. And at times tench will only feed once the sun is well up, and flooding into the swim from high above.

The summer is not always kind. In some years the weather grows hotter and hotter with air temperatures into the high eighties. No rain falls, the dew is burned off long before breakfast, and though thunder crackles occasionally, no storm breaks. The land is parched and the pastures turn brown. Crops are starved of water and the irrigation sprays belch forth all day long. Pools begin to retreat, lake levels drop, and rivers flow like canals. At best a lethargy creeps into the water and fish travel and feed less and less. More worrying, oxygen can fall to unacceptable levels, especially at nights in the weedy shallows where the plants absorb whatever is available. This is when the stressed, or sickly, or aged fish will die and when the stunted population of farm pond roach, for example, will be pruned. Sometimes, therefore, Nature is simply clearing out the dross; at others, the loss is tragic; at worst the drought sees whole pools turn to puddles and then to mud. Even if the fish are saved, their home is almost always lost, for once a bed cracks then any rain, however, torrential, will simply drain through uselessly and do nothing to bring back aquatic life. Of course, pools have come and gone for centuries. It is simply that today, with increased demands on springs and rivers from industry, agriculture and domestic usage, the process is speeded up and a drought will herald the demise of waters not yet ready to die naturally.

Nevertheless a pond that weathers the bad times and survives might well be in a position to flourish when the rains do come. The bed that has been long exposed becomes a haven for insects, and when fresh, oxygenated water floods in the fish are energised to make the very most of the revival. Weight is readily packed on and even old, seemingly tired fish can catapult forward in weight and condition—especially if the water's population was thinned out in the drought.

Many summers, though, are cool and damp, and these conditions also bring their problems. The survival rate of fry and fingerlings is reduced, and recruitment can be poor; this can be a blessing in a heavily stocked water, but a setback in a fish-poor one. Struggling populations need a strong year class sooner rather than later, and every unproductive year that passes decreases the chance of the purely natural recovery. The mortality rate of mature fish rises, and as older specimens are less fertile than those in the prime of life, fewer and fewer eggs are successfully produced. It can happen then that a series of cold summers actually spells the end of a fish population in a water. The few remaining adults just cannot sustain their numbers and their whole line dies out. This is tragic, especially as rarer fish like rudd are particularly vulnerable to weather patterns and can disappear without trace from a water.

A miserable summer also depresses waterfowl populations. Not only are there fewer fingerlings for the fish-eaters, but rain and cold winds can destroy whole broods of chicks. A wet fledgling just cannot get warm or dry and pathetic corpses of coot and heron chicks frequently litter the windward shore.

Poor summer weather does little to stimulate feeding, and just as water can become too warm so it can be too cold for any sustained feeding spells. Mild wet weather after a hot period can be excellent, but if one cold wet front follows another, the temperature falls quickly and so does fish activity. River fish are marginally less affected since water temperatures rarely exceed 60°F anyway, but even they feed less regularly and less hard.

There is now no doubt that low pressure itself badly affects feeding fish, and in virtually all cases a falling barometer will switch fish off most activity: the more dramatic the depression, the more complete the turn-off becomes. Frequently conditions seem to be ideal, yet still the fish don't feed. The reason? Approaching rapidly is a front bringing cold, wet, windy weather, and somehow the fish can already detect the weather change. How they do this is a mystery, but it does point to their acute sensitivity, and an awareness of minute changes in their environment that we, as the hunters, would do well to consider. Quite why a depression does have this effect is not clear, but certainly an entire water will go dead as the glass falls: waterfowl are less active, and even tiny water creatures like the water-boatman and the pond-skater appear to move less. Damselflies and dragonflies keep off the water surface, and fewer nymphs come up to hatch. In all probability, fish simply reflect this general slowing down in the life of the water around them, and respond by moving and feeding less themselves.

Rainfall is not always detrimental to the summer waters. Mild, overcast days with intermittent showers can see a great deal of feeding, especially if there is a little breeze and a clammy type of heat. Gentle rain overnight that ceases around dawn often stimulates heavy feeding in the early morning. Again, steady warm daytime rain that drifts away towards sunset will often result in wild activity at dusk. If the air is warm there will often be huge fly hatches, especially of adult common gnats emerging from their pupal cases; sometimes the hatch is so immense that the discarded cases stick to the line and make angling difficult, if not impossible.

The violent rain of a thunderstorm can also prove to be very beneficial, especially if the weather preceding it has been particularly hot. The downpour will reduce water temperatures to a more comfortable level, increase the oxygen content and can, if heavy enough, give a clear water a tinge of colour. The hours following a storm can, therefore, see frenzied feeding, especially from carp in shallow waters where the effect is all the more noticeable.

Autumn

It is quite usual for the autumn to begin with a long, lingering Indian summer that can last well into October. These are beautiful, rich, mellow days, and because it is on the wane, the warmth seems even more precious. Indeed, sometimes in the mid-afternoon it seems that true summer has never left. But there are differences in the water scene. The early mornings, for example, are damp and misty. The spider's hammock-like cobwebs, slung up by the riverside and amongst the tall yellow grasses, are weighed down with pearly beads of moisture. Even at midday a walk on some of the marshes or a visit through the wood to the pools mean being drenched with dew. The blue haze which all day hangs over the water is denser somehow than it was during the summer. It is as though Nature puts a thicker veil over her fading face. When the reeds rustle in the wind, it is with a crispness that already speaks of the reed cutter's harvest to come.

The days are becoming rapidly shorter, and the sunsets do not linger but go out in a quicker blaze. Night-times possess more than a summer chill to them, and can dip down towards freezing point, even after the very mildest of days. As a result, water temperatures are less stable and are beginning their gradual decline towards winter levels. Visibly the waterside is changing too, albeit slowly. The trees are still more green than gold, the weed is slowly receding and the reedbeds remain unbowed, but the tall willowherbs have burst their long seedpods and smothered themselves with clinging down. The river ditches are full of withered water parsnip and loosestrife, and that rather dull burr-marigold is almost the only flower in bloom—apart from meadowsweet which, in spite of its fragile appearance, here and there displays a cluster of blooms.

Insect life is also showing a gentle downturn. However, the damsel- and dragonflies still perch on the red-tip float from mid-morning; some mosquito larvae still hatch out, and algae and water-fleas still cover a great deal of the shallower areas.

All species of fish are feeding well. There is still plenty of food to stimulate them and water temperatures are still comfortable, even if falling. Very probably the fish are also aware that the leaner days of winter are approaching, and this knowledge does stimulate concentrated feeding. October is probably the best month for carp, bream, barbel, rudd and roach; in all probability it would be the same for tench if more anglers bothered to fish for them. This is a time when previously uncatchable fish seem to lose their caution and fall for larger food items which they gorge on in their eagerness to build up winter fat.

The early days—or rather nights—of October are probably just about the best possible time to mount a bream quest. It is dark early and a session lasting between 5 and 10pm will coincide with a feeding spell. This is all the more hectic if there is good cloud cover, a warm wind and a full or a new moon. We have long known that these two lunar phases influence the earth, its water and the behaviour of both humans and animals. New and full moons are caused by the sun and the moon being in alignment, and their combined gravitational pull actually causes inland waters to rise and fall in a small way, exactly like miniature tides on the sea. At the same time, the chemical and electrical balances of living creatures are altered: in us, this leads to more mental disturbance, more births and more sexual activity; in fish, this energy is directed towards feeding and if at the same time conditions are suitable as well, carp and bream especially may feed in a frenzy. It must be added that a full moon on a clear October night is less satisfactory—in all likelihood temperatures will drop quickly and the unfettered light of a full moon is probably too bright in clear cold water for the big-eyed bream to feed with confidence.

The predators, too, are especially busy, making the most of this last spell of plenty before the cold, the dark and the restricted activity of winter. After all, fish swimming close to the surface and intent upon their food make easier targets than those hugging the bottom in the dark, often holding up tight in to snags.

Perch feed upon several small fish rather than a single larger one, and this period suits them well. Shoals of small fish need to work harder for their food as the banks of water-fleas reduce, and therefore they travel more in their searches. This makes them more vulnerable, especially as the weedbeds are dying back somewhat, making it harder for a shoal of fish to hide effectively. The October light also suits hunting perch well: summer brilliance has waned and in this more shadowy water an approach on prey is made with less chance of alarming them.

This golden period changes abruptly with the first serious frost of the autumn. Within days the whole waterside world changes. The warblers are gone from the reedbeds and the wagtails from the river drains. The swallows, swifts and martins have followed them, along with whitethroats and wheatears. The trees, apart from the oaks, have begun to shed their leaves in earnest, and there is no doubt that as these rot they sour the water to some degree, especially if they are coated with dust or traces of chemical and toxin. The dense clumps of fungi and puffballs that have sprung up in the warm, damp weather blacken overnight, and in the water, lilybeds die back quickly now so that fish like crucian carp and rudd lose a lot of the shade they take confidence in. All forms of waterweed begin a fast decline and the waters become clearer, emptier, more unfriendly places. At the same time, reeds begin to turn gold, then brown and then fall and decay. The descent of water temperatures continues apace, especially when the margins are coated with cat-ice until sun up.

Fishing now takes a real knock. Everything slows down, especially whilst a period of blue skies and cold nights and high pressure persists. Most species now feed in shorter bursts, often just after darkness until just around 8 or 10pm. Daytime fishing is usually a waste of time on the stillwaters, though the river will still produce chub or dace through the daylight hours.

Carp are often visible if the water is clear enough and they tend to hang near the bottom, in amongst branches or decaying weed. They are far from being in a comatose state for they are still moving and their pectorals keep a steady beat; their eyes rotate and it is usual to see them suck in any suspected food. However, all these movements are gentle and docile and done at an easy pace. It is the start of a gradual drift towards the lethargy of winter.

If you wish to keep the carp feeding through the colder weather to come, now is the time to begin feeding them artificially on baits. Failure to do so means that as natural foods fall away, the carp become less and less dependent on feeding and, in fact, less inclined to do so at all. Careful, restricted feeding on as near to a daily basis as possible ensures that the carp are expecting food and looking for it, long after the bloodworms, the water-fleas, the water-shrimps and all their natural larder has already disappeared.

It is common for this particular period to end with the gales of late October and early November. These come with such ferocity that every remnant of summer is destroyed overnight. The trees are finally stripped. What remains of the lilies is pulled up and thrown to destruction, and the dead rushes are flattened and submerged. This is when tree damage is most common: some trees, especially the oak, still bear a few leaves that can offer a fatal resistance to the gales passing through the branches. After a night's storm, the water world wakes to the winter. The high winds are almost always accompanied by heavy rain that raises stillwater levels and, if sufficiently prolonged, will colour and even flood the rivers. Though the rain is cold, if anything, it does improve prospects. Adding some colour to the water is often enough to stimulate fish that have not fed for a while. Furthermore the influx of rainwater also cleans out stale, leaf-poisoned lakes and rivers.

As the storm subsides the weather generally remains disturbed, cloudy and frequently quite mild: in short, conditions that often witness the very last, very short serious feeding spell before true winter sets in. Carp, tench and rudd especially are jolted into fresh life and will feed hard as long as this particular weather pattern lasts.

Often this is not long enough. Generally the wind from the west gradually dies and there will be a period of calm. Imperceptibly at first, but its influence growing all the time, the wind now comes in from the north or the east and feels much colder. The blanket grey of the sky breaks up and clear patches start to appear. The wind rises, grows colder and if a shower breaks, it probably falls as sleet rather than rain. The whole water world shudders. The winter bird migrants have arrived, the widgeon, the pochards and even skuas and kittiwakes. The valley looks grey, and the fish have settled into a life of stupefied lethargy punctuated by only bursts of half-hearted feeding. Winter is here.

START OF THE YEAR

— *Arctic Winters* —

So, this is the tale of one year in the life of a particular valley. A more water-splashed region is hard to imagine which as far as I am concerned is why it is such a vibrant place, the differing character of its waters offering a unique variety of plant and animal life.

My story begins in the winter, though by necessity a relatively brief introduction, for this is the period when water is most dormant. For many species, the cold months are always a time of intermittent sleep and frequently

A gloomy day in the winter as the wind begins to rise in the west and pushes ever-gathering clouds before it. The temperature, however, will probably rise and there is every chance that once the worst of the rain has passed over the fish will begin to feed in earnest

winter weather makes observation, and therefore a deeper understanding of their life cycle, almost impossible. This was particularly so during the year in question. The weather conditions between January and March were some of the most violently changing ones I personally have known. The new year was ushered in with violent gales: a deep depression had gathered in mid-Atlantic and tracked to our shores, arriving in the early hours of one particular January day. I awoke two hours before dawn, aroused by the noise of the most terrible winds around the house and in the wood. It was hardly safe to venture out, but I felt bound to investigate: straightaway I found dead pigeons scattered in the half light—they would be eaten by foxes, badgers and stoats within twenty-four hours. Despite the storm the moon still rode high, throwing a ghostly sheen of light over the scene of violence and noise. The roof of our cottage seemed to rise and fall at every blast, the tiles rattling in the wild wind.

I felt it safer to leave the wood, and moved out into the meadows. Half a mile away lay Gallows Hill pond, in desperate danger of breaking its dam as the wind threw the water against the ancient rampart of crumbling stone and brickwork. In the growing light I patched up the ever-narrowing bank as best I could with sods of earth and bricks from the old estate walls. Sunrise was unearthly, the cloud and the rain obscuring any real light, yet shafts of yellow occasionally breaking through. It was then that carp began to leap, roughly shaken out of their winter torpor. I took a water temperature and found it had risen six degrees since morning the previous day. Satisfied that the pool was safe, I continued my way down the valley. There were fallen trees everywhere, great oaks, alders, and a willow that had been flung a hundred yards from the river course. I passed a barn with its roof torn off, and the keeper's cottage which was missing a chimney stack and all its old fencing.

But it was down at the coast that the worry was greatest. In 1953 a gale no worse than this present one had combined with a spring tide so that the defences were breached and the sea had rushed in. Houses were destroyed, ships were carried two miles inland, people and livestock had to be rescued or were lost: almost forty years on this was still a time remembered with fear and distress. I climbed the shingle beach and found the wind coming due north, stinging my eyes; birds were tossed in a dark and ominous sky, and the sea in front of me raged yards higher than the marshlands beneath—but there was still a safety margin. A group of fishermen informed me that the tide was past its height and so the worst was over, though they had the prudence to keep the sandbags in place around their doors.

So this short day was spent in great anxiety, clearing trees and watching the waters with a great deal of concern. I feared for the old boathouse at the Bream Lake, but although slates were thrown high by the wind and the oak pillars bent and groaned to each blast, they were held firm by footings that went several feet down through the silt and into the chalk of the lake bed. The structure would survive.

At the Buddha's lake the water lay strangely calm and serene, protected by the high banks and the tall trees that swayed above it—the scene could even have been peaceful but for the occasional roar as a bough was flung from one of the surrounding oak trees.

A sad testament to the storm

The tide simply swept in that terrible night and deluged the village. It swept over the road in the top right of the photograph and then spread out, totally submerging the river valley and the farm land. The saltwater devastated as it flooded. Worms and moles, freshwater fish and sheep, cattle and human beings—all perished before the onslaught. Only the eels escaped, woken from their winter sleep and seen escaping with the ebb

The river took the full force of the wind along its south to north course. It was very clear, in spite of a surface distorted by waves, and in the deeper pools roach could be seen, especially when the odd glimpse of sunlight appeared through the racing clouds. They were quite still, lying close to the river bed, hidden by the dead weed around them. They could have been logs. They were, I guessed, all but stunned by the drop in pressure that had spiralled endlessly downwards over the past twenty-four hours. Should the sea again break through the defences and rush up the river in a great salt flood there would be no escape for these comatose shoals—by the end of the storm they would be tears of silver on the marshes.

(opposite) *The hurricane winds collapse an old building entirely. Beneath the scattered pantiles the old straw can be seen clearly—a more hospitable nesting place for mice and birds than felt can ever be* (opposite) *This lake froze within hours of the cold weather arriving. There was no wind whatsoever and the ice lies as flat as a pane of glass and just as clear. Soon it will be possible to walk on it and view fish lying quietly beneath*

Sometime around sunset a crack in the clouds allowed the light to shine through, and as the skies cleared so the wind dropped. The stars came out hard and cold, obviously heralding a new phase of weather. I made up the fire and went to bed quite happy, pleased that the roof had held and that the woods and the waters had largely escaped serious damage. The night was very still and silent as a hard frost began to fall, and by morning it was a different view through the window, a white world, as quiet as the previous day had been violent. I walked out along the frozen cart track to Gallows Hill and found the pond there skimmed right over. Even the larger lakes were fringed with ice. The sky was at first lemon and then blue as the weak sun pulled his way through the heavens.

Already there was the sound of chainsaws in the wood, and the smoke of fires and the smell and crackle of burning scrub. All the waters, however, were again

The typical start of cold weather. The skies clear and take on a luminous blue by day and a starlit silver by night. The ground is frozen and skimmed with frost, ready to receive and hold the snows as they fall. This is a desperate time for wildlife particularly, and even fish can suffer should the bad weather continue over-long

settling down after the battering of the storm, and soon everything would drift back to its own type of sleep again: the pike that had been raised to a last meal; the roach that had hurried to feed off the windward shore; the bream shoal that had begun to cloud the water in feeding frenzy; even the tench that had opened one of his little red eyes—all pulled the blanket of winter over themselves again.

The hard, dry weather lasted one month, and the ice thickened and the ground became iron hard. It was now quite possible to walk on the lakes and look through ice that was window-clear to the waters beneath. Most days I went to check up on the Buddha—'my' fish, a huge, rounded, smooth brown leather carp that I had 'discovered' and watched until it had become almost a friend. Now, it hung like a battleship, always over one area of its small water, possibly where a spring flowed in warm and fresh with oxygen. The wild carp at Gallows Hill too were plainly visible, most days moving slightly and obviously feeding with mild intent. The river was reduced to an ever-narrowing channel flowing between encroaching ice sheets. Sometimes when the midday sun was warm enough, lumps of this ice would break away and bob down the stream off to the sea where the salt would eventually melt it. The only fish it was possible to catch in these conditions were the dace, darting like silver fingers after the falling maggots. The roach shoals were totally lost in the gloom in the deep bends in the pools: during the day they shunned the brightness of the blue sky, only feeding after dark or when there was a cloud over the moon. Though I tried to fish for them during these times the cold was so piercingly intense that after less than an hour I would be driven indoors.

Even the mud-flats where the river flowed into its estuary were frozen. At first the lugworm diggers went out each low tide but so miserable a number of worms did they collect that at last they gave up and spent their days in front of their fires at home or in The Swallows. Indeed, later on in the month the cold became so extreme that the mudflats and sands froze hard as soon as the tides uncovered them and any digging was quite futile. Naturally, this weather had dire effects on bird life. Small waders became so weak that they were easy prey for the hungry hooded crows and black-backed gulls. Brent geese became completely fearless, and as the marshes remained frozen, most of the moorhens began to die of hunger. Marshes and meadows saw a terrible number of deaths: bitterns and herons perished and water-rails were amongst the first to succumb to the cold—fifteen were found dead where the river moved to sea. In the little harbour they were seen attacking starving dunlin and even feeding on the corpse of a coypu. Wrens were frozen to death on the very coldest night and the species will almost certainly be hard hit for years to come. Those that huddled together in large enough numbers for warmth survived—forty wrens roosted in a single nesting-box in the wood near the cottage.

The gardens in the village were invaded by a huge number of redwings, fieldfares and blackbirds. Many existed on spoiled apples left over from the bumper harvest of the autumn. People of the village saw all manner of strange sights: a kestrel attacked a woodcock in flight, and a water-rail which had

Cold so intense that buckets of water freeze within minutes and the ice on small ponds is an inch thick

The reed cutters are at work with the windmill again in the background

swooned in a coma was found to have its belly feathers encased in ice. It was thawed out and fed on worms, accepting these fearlessly from the fingers of a longshore fisherman. At the coast, a number of fieldfares survived for a while by pecking frozen carrots from the fields. However, in the end they became feeble in the extreme; many of those clustering around a waterhole in the ice of a marsh dyke were blown in by the bitter east wind, and all were drowned. The keeper did his best: finding three half-starved bitterns, he cared for them in a pen, feeding them mainly on sprats. He it was who saw a dying mute swan killed and devoured by a fox; and who spread out 4cwt of apples in his garden to be devoured by blackbirds, song thrushes, fieldfares, redwings, bramblings and tits. Reed-cutting continued during this period, but this time workers often noted that normally shy birds began to follow them for food. Crumbs of bread, cheese and cake were greedily gobbled down by bearded tits that usually would not come within yards of them.

Then sadly, after weeks of this frost, snow began to fall. In a single night twelve inches gathered, more where the slight wind had piled it against the

(opposite) *The lugworm diggers go out immediately the tide ebbs and leaves the mudflats exposed. Very cold weather, however, sends the worms down deep and soon digging becomes totally fruitless*

A strong breeze has kept the lake ice-free for the time being, but if the sky clears around full moon the temperatures will drop and the water will freeze, corrugated by the wind

(opposite) *The untrodden snow lies thick beyond the gate to the village*

(opposite) *The upper river in the spring still looks bleak, but nature is on the move again*

remnants of the deer fence around my wood. First the gales and then the ice and now the snow: all resulted in a terrible time for the valley. The lakes were barely distinguishable from the fields under this mantle of white. Occasional areas of watery slush showed where a feeder stream entered, or a powerful spring filtered through the ice and warmed the area. No real light entered the water, and life ticked on at its lowest ebb. No longer could I watch the Buddha or the wild carp, and even travelling to the river now became hazardous; at its peak I was snowed into the cottage for a week, and during that time saw only one person stumbling along two fields away, almost waist deep in white. I did what I could to help the birds and animals in the surrounding woods, for now snow was covering windfall apples and all remaining food—within only a few days a whole congregation of creatures gathered each morning for whatever I could produce for them. My supplies quickly grew low and eventually I had to risk a journey to the nearest shop three miles away, by foot, over the whitened landscape. Stale bread, potato peelings, carrot tops, apple cores— anything and everything would be eaten by the starving hordes.

This final stage continued for nearly another four weeks, and it was well into March before the winter began to loosen its grip. Then at last, longer days and a warmer sun began to work their magic: within a week the snow had all but gone, only lingering in the deepest darkest hollows, and the ice that was over a foot deep began very gradually to melt away. Each day I walked the banks of the river, the streams, the pools and the lakes with ever-growing anxiety, not having any way of knowing whether the fish had survived or what casualties there would be when the ice finally cleared. Each day seemed to produce a new sadness: a rotted heron, a still frozen stoat or the ghostly shape of a belly-up bream beneath the ice. I tried to be philosophical during these days and reasoned that the weather was Nature's way of purging out the weak and perhaps thinning back populations that had outgrown their resources. There had been other terrible winters, and the valley had recovered and flourished after those. Accepting the inevitable purpose of this terrible winter helped a little, but it was still with great anxiety that I awaited the spring.

The springtime mole pokes his nose into the milder air

A Friend From Childhood

There was a knock at the cottage door late one night. It was Don, come unexpectedly from the city, where he had lost his job, his flat, his girlfriend . . . all his reasons for staying there. So, in a time of crisis, he had returned to the valley. I had known Don as a boy, fished with him throughout our teens and for those few precious weeks of holiday each year. I had always been sorry that his brains and his ambitions had taken him to the city, for I had always felt sure his contribution to the sport could have been immense. I also felt, in my own countrified smugness, that he was missing some of the richness of life. Now, it was marvellous to see him so unexpectedly.

'Should I light a fire?' The house seemed cold to me awakening from a deep sleep. 'Not for me. I'm fine. Look, I'm sorry, I should have called you. It's not on, barging in like this.'

Opening a bottle of burgundy convinced him I did not mind, and as I lit the fire he unfolded all the thoughts that had been troubling him.

'I'm here now for a long while,' he said. 'Things have been up and down recently and this place is what I need. I want to immerse myself in all those things I've started here over the years and had to leave unfinished, things I've found wonderful and inexplicable.' He brooded. 'This estate, the whole valley, it's always been magic.' Another pause. 'Well, now I'm here. The flat's for sale and I reckon I've enough cash to do nothing for a year but fish, wander, learn, and work things out.' He laughed. 'And what's happening up here? How have things been?'

I told him of the bad winter, of the cold spring and my fears for the fish. 'And what of the Buddha?' he asked. I shrugged. 'He's not been seen since the end of January.' 'Alive?' 'I should think so. There weren't any big fish found.' 'Gallows Hill?' 'That's fine now. We had a bit of a scare during the gales but everything's fine.' 'And the river?' 'The same. It's all amazing when you think what we've gone through. I don't think anything significant has been lost. The birds took a hammering I'm sad to say, and some of the wildlife was thinned out a bit, but the fish seem to have survived remarkably well.'

At 2am I made some fried eggs; not that I was hungry but I guessed he would be ravenous. And more than that, the meal was a resurrection of old ritual, of late night fishing sessions that always ended around a kitchen table. We would be gravel-eyed, cold, hungry, elated or near despair but deep down happy always to be fishermen.

We talked of the 1950s and the 1960s, when we had discovered new waters and new methods, of long summer holidays when home was merely a bed and we would be away at dawn, cycling five, ten or fifteen miles up and down the full extent of the valley. It was a life of sandwiches, of strawberries from the field and fruit from the orchards, days of delicious freedom.

Spring comes at last to the Rectory stream in the wood. Everything was late but Nature has this way of speeding herself up and atoning so that by May the savage winter is well forgotten

The fishing then, and this type of life, were equally rich. Fishing pressure up and down the valley, and throughout the whole country, was minimal and many good waters were barely touched after the first few days of the season in early June. A loaf of bread was all the carp bait that was ever needed and even fish that were considered wary then were quite happy to take lumps of flake or paste from the bottom, or huge pieces of crust from the top. Bites too were utterly confident and developed into steady runs that just went and went till they were struck.

Nor were the fish tackle-shy, which was as well considering the comparatively poor quality of nylon which would sometimes lie like loops of wire along the bottom. Rods were either split or whole cane, or solid or hollow glass, and their action could be poker-like. Even the much sought after Mark IV, designed and built by Dick Walker, cast badly in the rain, though admittedly its action was magnificent. Methods were primitive by today's standards: the hair rigs, bolt rigs, confidence rigs and anti-eject rigs of today had not even been dreamed of.

However the lack of pressure on the bankside did have the effect of making the fish far more wary of an angler's presence than they might be today, when bivvies have become such a permanent feature that they will soon need planning permission! An angler's approach to the water had to be Apache-like, or fish of every species would just melt away. Camouflaged hats and clothing were designed and worn, and anglers often placed screens between themselves and the water. Noise had to be kept to a minimum, and every action was gentle and unhurried.

It is on the rivers, though, that the greatest changes have taken place over thirty years. Then shoals of roach that were literally a hundred or more yards long, and probably holding well over ten thousand fish, could be found dimpling the surface. When a pike hit into them, the water would lift up in a hail of silver and red and the roar could be heard far across the flood plains. Such shoals were common, and catches of a hundred or more roach were commonplace. So much competition for food made the fish easy to catch and baits and tackle and methods could all be very basic. Perch too were far more common than today and they could reach extraordinary sizes. Once an angler close to us caught a massive perch—I can see it now, from thirty odd years ago—and claimed that it weighed 6lb. Since that day Don and I have always assumed that we have at least *seen* a record perch in our lives, though it never occurred to us to try for one ourselves. 'Was it really 6lb?' Don asked now. 'We didn't see the man weigh it, did we? All I remember is that huge grey perch with the string through its gills hanging out in the sun over the railings.' 'I remember we both looked and looked,' I replied. 'I reckon we knew then that that perch was something we'd be lucky to see the like of again.'

Childhood is really the time when true anglers are made, and the magic of fishing to a boy is a spell that captivates for all time. Water is a mystery that will never be fully unravelled, and a fish is a triumph beyond all compare. Don and I were like all boys and had a strange closeness to fish that adults somehow lose. As boys we could visualise them exactly as they lay in the water, and I am now sure that a lot of our captures were due to this sixth sense. True to the age-old instinct for survival, perhaps our senses and our intuition are particularly sharp

*A massive perch is the very finest of any big fish and this is perch fishing in a frame.
The aggressive dorsal fin and gill cover both indicate a predator, and the small bait
lies beneath the perch, savagely scarred. Sadly above the ventral fin a lesion bubbles
out of the fish; the beginning of the infamous perch disease showing on this fine
specimen. In a matter of weeks or even days this fish could well be no more*

in childhood and only dull with age and increasing security. In some ways then
to be called childlike is the greatest compliment, and suggests a continuing
awareness that so many adults pretend to ignore.

I stoked the fire and we remembered the 1970s. 'They were good days,'
Don said, 'at least until I decided on my career.' 'Well, the travelling we did
away from here was good for us,' I replied. 'We learned a lot, even though I,
certainly, missed the valley at times. But you know, not everything here is like
it was. Everything changes. Anyway, let's leave all that for the time being. Just
what are you going to do right now?'

'Right,' Don said. 'I want a bed now, and a cottage as soon as possible! I'm
going to fish and fish, everything that has puzzled me in the past I'm going
to work out and explain. I'm going to know the waters in this valley like no
one ever before!'

And with that, he promptly fell asleep in the chair.

A Valley Changed

'You have got to realise,' I said the next morning, 'the valley isn't what it was. Take that little factory above the mill—that was probably the most dramatic problem we've seen. It turned out that it had been leaching chemicals into the river for years, and that's largely why the trout disappeared in the upper reaches and certainly why the roach declined lower down. Remember how I said that we were seeing otters less and less? Well, in the end, we were just finding corpses, animals that had died of blindness and cancers. One poor female was actually found running down the village street, half blind and bumping into cars and buildings. There was nothing anybody could do for her and she died in hours, full of cancer again. It was the tale of that otter that really caused a commotion. The press got hold of it and the factory was closed down. It was only a cowboy enterprise, a three-man unit, but the damage it had done was horrible.'

Once I started, I warmed to my theme. 'And nowadays there is far too much water being taken out of the ground. There are at least twice as many people in the valley as there were when we were children, and they have all got cars which they wash every week. There are washing machines and dish washers in every kitchen and of course at least two flush toilets to each house—it's estimated that now, every person in the valley uses sixty to seventy gallons of water every day. Thirty years back some people hardly used any at all. Do you remember old Lennie? How he would wear the same corduroy suit every day for seven years until it finally dropped to pieces when he'd throw it away and buy another one—and I doubt he ever washed or shaved. But though he might not have been a model of hygiene, the important thing is he certainly didn't plunder the water supplies!

'Agriculture has changed for the worse, too. I'm not saying the farmers are greedy . . . it's simply their business has intensified, like any other. But there are just too many boreholes now, and when we get a hot summer like last, they spray water all day long—potato crops are the worst and they just soak it up. The problem is that these boreholes tap right down into the water-table and wreak havoc with the springs. So what happens to all the spring-fed lakes that we have, up and down the valley? I'll tell you. The springs get weaker and weaker and inflowing water is reduced, so levels drop and silt builds up. Look at Gallows Hill—that was three feet deep when we were lads. Remember that carp that pulled your rod in and we had to wade after it? Well, it's only a foot deep now at the most, and shrinking each year. If these boreholes aren't contained then Gallows Hill and all the rest will be gone before long.

'Just as bad, the farmers have drained half the flood meadows—in fact that's an absolute disaster. You know, in winter the river would flood out and the meadows would hold the water like a giant sponge and release it back dribble by dribble throughout the summer. The river never threatened to run dry in those days like it did last year.

'And nobody then ever realised the implications of those new-fangled sprays—after every rain, more and more chemicals washing into the river. And that's combined with other horrors, too . . . the sewage plant, for example, I

This is a tragic photograph. It is taken in a spot where in the 1970s four feet of water ran over gravels, even at the height of summer in minimum rainfalls. This photograph was taken in January after a period of relatively heavy rain. The whole river has changed its character within twenty years. The banks have been dredged and canalised so that what water remains is channelled ever more swiftly out to sea and not allowed to linger and feed the ever-shrinking water table

Not even irrigation and boreholes can crucify all springs. Here is the king of them all, a fount of fresh, clear, cool water that feeds a Rectory stream through all conditions

The river begins to flood. Hopefully it will climb over its banks and settle in the meadows and ditches and linger on for several weeks until the whole land becomes like a sponge and can release water back slowly through the summer months when the rainfall is at its least and abstraction is at its height. Heavy winter rain is a necessity for the health of the river and the flood plains must be preserved

(opposite) The flood begins to break out over the river plains

The horrible effect of blanket weed in the river, a symptom of over-enrichment. Blanket weed has little nutritional value and harbours few insects of food forms. In the winter it breaks up and rolls down the river, making fishing almost impossible

happen to know has broken down at least half-a-dozen times in the last five years. Once it was disastrous, but only a few of us actually got to know about it and everything was hushed up. And in summer storms, think of all the lead and pollutants washing in from the roads. So in all, you've got some really lethal cocktails in the river. And what's the result? In a month or two when the water warms up there'll be great banners of that vile blanket weed all down the river. The ranunculus has gone, so has the startwort, and the gravels are all choked up—so where do the roach spawn and feed now? Not even the crayfish are safe. You won't believe it, but that crew from the new restaurant in the town were catching them and serving them up as starters!' Though they were prosecuted for it.

Don was looking ever more melancholy, but I hadn't finished.

'And we anglers have hardly helped ourselves, either. We allowed half the river to be electrofished, coarse fish to be carted off and rainbow trout to be put in their place, and what good do they do? They're either caught in days or they clear off to sea and end up in the seals. Worst still, carp seem to have gone into waters everywhere willynilly, whether they suited the water or not.

The seals lie on the sandbanks just out from the river's estuary. They have spent several hours feeding on mullet, bass and mackerel and perhaps the odd trout that has escaped the river confines and tried to make its way to the sea. Like so many other creatures in nature, these seals were recently threatened both by their own disease and by a mystery virus that killed several hundred. In all probability its cause was nothing more than stress, a result of increased commercial fishing and a decline in the fish population which in its turns created chronic food shortages for these creatures

Perfect design: the original carp. Muscle not fat. Speed not lumbering power that weight alone gives

The valley hasn't been too bad and those wildies still seem alright, but once there was a plan even there to stock with a few mirrors. Rudd, tench, crucian carp—they're all on the decline these days . . . So, just don't expect things to be like they were thirty years ago or you'll be disappointed.'

'Well, I've suspected at least half of all this,' said Don. 'But whatever has happened, and I appreciate it's bad, a lot of it, there are still fish worth catching in the valley, and there are still more challenges here than in most other places. And who knows, between us, we might even be able to get these issues better aired, perhaps even get something done about them. I know that wouldn't be easy, but we could at least try.'

Trying not to be cynical, I explained to him those problems facing any angler who wishes to change things for the better. Long experience of several water campaigns has shown that anglers do not have long patience spans away from the water's edge, and that after a few weeks' effort support begins to dribble away. Still, there have been successes in the past, and water quality has been improved by the combined effect of letters to MPs, news features on radio, television and in the national, local and angling press, of large public meetings and of petitions. The existence of a group of leaders who are not

The seals await on the sandbanks in the estuary, ever hungry, ever watchful for a meal of bass, mullet or even trout escaping the river and moving into the salt environment

afraid of bureaucracy and so-called experts is vital. These people must be committed, articulate, efficient organisers and fully conversant with the issues that face them. There will be a lot of pressure on them from authority on the one side and from the anglers on the other, and unpopularity comes far more quickly and easily than praise. Providing Don realised all this, with his business expertise, there would be every chance that he could be a real asset in helping champion the angler's cause.

I soon found a cottage for him, only a short walk through the wood, on the way to Gallows Hill. It was small, dark, damp, rough and Don loved it. He signed a year's lease and paid the whole amount in £50 notes, unprecedented on the estate where rents are normally a month late at least! It was very sparsely furnished, which Don claimed to like, claiming that it would be good for him finally to shake off the shackles of capitalism and to get back to nature and appreciate the things that were truly important.

When I visited him in his new home, we had a dinner of sorts from a cooker that seemed to work at half power, in the company of legions of mice which were busily active once the gloomy dusk had set in. 'Right,' he said, all brisk and efficient, 'tomorrow we get to look at the lot. It will be the first of June and we'll be out from dawn. This is the start of my new life!'

VALLEY CARP

He was awake at ten, just in time to walk to Gallows Hill before lunch! It was a better sort of day altogether, the sun quite powerful and the sky blue and clear. The path ahead was shot with shadow and light as it snaked deeper and deeper into ancient oak wood. New nettles crowded over for the way was little used, and Don and I walked in single file. Years of neglect had served the estate's wildlife well. Fields were farmed but they were broken up by large tracts of woodland that were not much disturbed in any way. Shooting had all but ceased since the last keeper had died, and money had not been found to replace him. There were two foresters but they could barely keep pace and the woods became increasingly tangled. Every type of wild animal flourished: the sand and gravel banks favoured the rabbits and foxes, whilst the highest rise of dry earth riddled with tree roots had been a major sett for half a century. Now it honeycombed out for almost an acre and was home to a dozen badgers. The estate's deer park had declined between the wars, the fences had collapsed and the deer gradually escaped. Their ancestors lived on, in the woods by day, grazing the fields by night. In the February just past I had fed half a dozen beasts on vegetable scraps during the worst two weeks of the winter.

After ten minutes walk we came to the meadow and crossed it to the pond that lay in its middle. The carp were busy working around the margins and we settled down to watch them. The lake had not been disturbed for a year to my knowledge and the fish were quite oblivious to our presence. One swam so close to the margin its back and forehead were well clear of the water. It was a classic wild carp—long and lean and grey in colour—a fish type that has been in England for 800 years at least and is quite different from the foreign imports of the last half century or so. One of us shifted and the carp torpedoed off, leaving a furrowed brow as it sped. Imagine a light rod bent to that fish!

The rest of the fish around, though, fed on. With their heads they burrowed into the soft mud, digging out the midge larvae. Bubbles rose from their gill flaps and the mud cloud billowed around each fish as its fins worked to keep the body in position and to give little surges of power that drove the head ever deeper into the lake bed. Feeding in this way is a demanding process—every fibre, every fin is being used constantly for food returns which are, per individual, very small. In large part, this helps explain the extreme slimness of the wild carp: centuries of interbreeding between arrow-shaped ancestors and the constant hard work required just to survive, have combined to produce these greyhound fish.

Also, the wildie is a product of the shallow pool, of waters that bake in summer and can resemble permafrost in the winter. Only three months back Gallows Hill had been solid to the very silt under a hat of snow two feet deep. At the time it seemed quite impossible that any fish would survive; but now,

The Observatory Tower commands a view out to sea and across the entire estate to the village and the coast. In part its purpose was to watch for any rising of the labouring classes during periods of discontent so that the Hall servants could be gathered into some type of home guard

(opposite above) The sparrowhawks nest in the pine forest where they can raise their brood in comparative safety and with a sure supply of food

(opposite below) A picture from the past when the estate was keepered and stoats were killed in numbers to protect the pheasant chicks. Rooks, crows, magpies, weasels, owls and all birds of prey were ruthlessly sacrificed to protect the sport of the gentry. These ghastly gibbets are ever more a sight of the past

The sleek form of a typical wild carp

Wild carp very active in shallow water, burrowing for food and even coming half clear of the water to take insects off the overhanging reed stems

A large wild carp back well clear of the water as it forages for bloodworm in the silt

without a casualty, the wild carp were feeding and, by the look of things, preparing to spawn. In groups of two, three and four, carp were chasing round the pool, kicking up mud and disturbing the more solemn feeders. In a frenzy, one fish actually grounded himself momentarily on a mud bank way out in the middle of the pool. That was how shallow the lake had now become and I could see the concern on Don's face. In fact the drinking place where the bullocks kept the silt well in check had become the deepest part of the entire water. It was no wonder, then, that the herons were gathering there each dawn in increasing numbers. The wonder was that the fish should continue to survive and thrive.

It was hardly surprising that no other species of fish could maintain an existence in such a shrunken water. What roach there had been died out years back, and even the stock of tench had gradually petered out, starved of oxygen in the summer and hit by long winter freezes. Even the eels had all but disappeared, unable to hide effectively from herons in such shallow water. Just one of two remained, big, cunning eels that spent the daylight hours around the fallen fencing in the middle of the lake and only left shelter to feed at night.

The absence of other fish undoubtedly benefited the carp by giving them sole right to the food stocks of the little lake. The decrease in depth did also allow the water to warm up quickly in the spring, and therefore proliferate with bloodworm. The daily addition of waste from the drinking cattle only made

The Gardener's Lake nestles in its little fold in the hills. Far away the sea is just visible beyond the oak woods. In places trees and reeds crowd around giving a large fish perfect sanctuary

conditions even more perfect for the worms' growth. Providing the carp could find enough water to cover their gills then there was never the chance that they would go hungry. Numbers of fish had fallen away since our childhood days partly because weed growth had become non-existent, and spawning had necessarily suffered. The small carp that did hatch out were also easy prey for the herons which decimated recruitment.

Rumours

Don had made surprising headway with the house so as to be all ready for the 16 June, the opening of the fishing season still a few days away. One evening we walked through the woodland, down the track to The Swallows, a good way off but the weather was fine and the night would be light. We had not gone far before he asked the one question I had been anticipating for some time, and rather feared.

'And the Buddha, John? What are your plans?'

I answered, 'I haven't seen him myself this spring but the gardener says he's been about. At times I was worried in the winter, of course, but I looked round carefully after the thaw and saw no signs of disaster.'

'You needn't worry, you know, I shall leave him to you. You've done the work on him, though I'll watch and listen if I may.'

I was both grateful and ashamed. The Buddha was 'my' fish on one level, since I had after all found him; but what man can own a fish that he has not caught? What right does a man have to any life in the wild? The Buddha had given me enough already—simply finding him had been a challenge.

In the valley, as everywhere, stories were told. No harm was meant by them, and they were in fact a reflection of ordinary country people's interest in the world around them, an interest more like a passion really, that could stir the imagination and sway reason. Truth at best is a murky commodity and what people actually think, and think they see, often becomes fact in itself. My interest in fishing was well known, and everyone would make an effort to please, telling of first- or second-hand experiences, of tails seen and tales of grandfather fish heard. A big fish to most people is anything over two feet in length, and thereafter the scale of vastness is largely unimportant. There was no desire to deceive me, and the general distortions simply reflected generosity of spirit, and enthusiasm for the valley and its mysteries. Further, there was an element of pride in some of the storytellers: those of the valley loved it deeply, and their wish was simply to paint it in its most glorious colours, quite capable of holding all treasures.

Therefore I could easily have believed that the great carp of the Gardener's Lake was a fantasy, its size imagination—the pool itself was created more for ornamentation than for any serious sporting purpose and was less than an acre in extent. Yet it was in places deep and the water was rich and fertile, and since big fish water has its own character, I did not dismiss the pool giant out of hand. Water that pulses to daphne and water fleas; that is crystal clear but so packed with life that you can never see to the bottom, where big fish are

A deep, dark wood still keeps its mysteries and its night-time voices. The path to the Buddha runs through one of these enchanted places

occasionally glimpsed and small fish seem absent; waters where the only sign of life is the mysterious stirring of a weedbed, the sudden eruption of a sheet of bubbles, or at dead of night a roar of spray in the silence: such a water was the Gardener's Lake.

In my early investigations I hardly understood estate lakes at all. I did not realise that the quieter the water the more difficult it is to approach, that a human presence is detected in some strange unknown way and not necessarily actually seen or heard. The heavy footfall, the long shadow, the excited voice are not fatal in themselves for a big fish will already be aware and will have become invisible. Even if you creep and crawl, hide behind trees, stalk like a heron or move like a ghost, carp will fade from the scene. It is just as though the toads tell them.

One humid day I spent watching the Gardener's Lake, seeing occasional hints of fish, but these were so slight and so subtle they could easily have been imagination. Was that shadow fish, or bird, or flutter of my eyelid? Surely those large lazy bubbles came from the gills of a carp. Or were they from the stirring of rotten leaves under the sway of the wind or the coil of an eel? That lily must have folded before a fin. Or could it have been the breeze? Was that puff of clouded water stirred up by a carp or the dabchick that lived in the alders?

(opposite) *An old and fertile pond, still enriched by springs and the dribble from the hill's plumbing system. The condition produces rich weed growth and big fish*

Another visit on a still grey morning. The lake rocked but there was no wind. The flow stirred but there wasn't even a breeze, and everything was very quiet. There was no sunrise for the cloud canopy was too thick and the sky simply lightened rapidly, until even this was checked abruptly by a cover of black driven from the west. The rain rodded down and the rabbits fled to the warm earth. Finally it was light again but this time with a slight breeze, the lake surface a clear mirror. At last came a fleeting ray of sunlight through a bar of cloud. Now, those, surely, were fish bubbles. They came up with a ferocity that literally fizzed them around the float, stirring it, lifting it at their climax. And the bubbles had a course to them, a defined straight movement from left to right across the clearing in the weeds.

The float twitched. Positive rings radiated from it. It cocked but lay flat again instantly. My hand trembled on the rod butt but there was nothing more. This was a fish, no doubt, but a great carp, or a tench or even an eel up from the sea I could not tell. Had the line caught around the flank or a fin, or had a mighty fish sampled the bait a second and found something of distaste in it? The morning wore on and confidence wore away.

Strings of bubbles begin to lace the water around the float. They follow a very positive course and this alone suggests that a fish has to be responsible

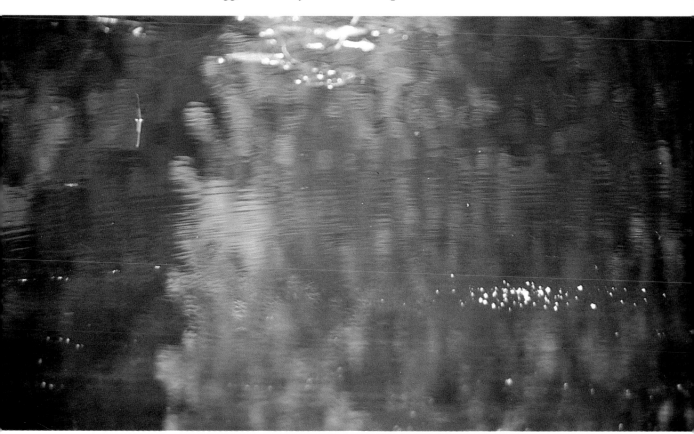

Oh yes, they were there, the gardener himself kept telling me. He'd see them from the greenhouses when the sun shone and one of them . . . well, she was no rumour. Good weather came and I saw six carp myself over a spell of a few days, very nice fish indeed, all in the teens and pretty neat-looking, leathery fish with no visible signs of past damage. These would more than do for me and I set about catching the occasional one without too much effort. All in all, I hugely enjoyed the lake without ever really feeling I could truly be on the verge of anything notably special.

Then one very warm day I had fallen asleep down at the shallow end, on a slightly raised grass bank where a stream enters over rocks. When eventually I did wake, I did not move at first but lay still, my eyes only gradually opening and staring wider and wider. Ten yards from my nose lay the rumour, every ounce of her. For pectorals she had two great coral pink tennis rackets and her mouth was a tunnel. She was a foot longer at least than any other fish I had seen in the lake, and half as broad again. She bellied sideways and her depth, too, was enormous. This fish was flesh and blood and our relationship had truly begun.

A perfect mirror carp. Its fins are immaculate, but above all its body shows no sign of the barrel-shaped obesity that is so common with recently imported genetic types. This particular fish is the progeny of an old stocking of slim but beautifully proportioned carp that frequently made 25 or even 30 pounds in weight.

The Buddha

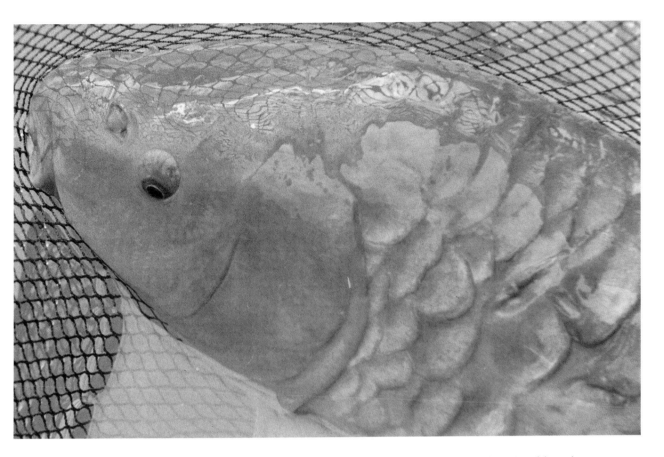

It is easy to believe in the supernatural wisdom of a carp when you look at its old and wise brow. Certainly the fish may be old and may be very wary of an intrusion into its environment

Since Don had given me the monopoly on the Buddha, all I now had to do was to catch him: but if Don were to have his problems that summer, then so was I! Some say that small waters are no challenge, that they are claustrophobic; yet they are the only places where a big fish can be seen constantly, and perhaps be deeply or truly understood. Certainly for four months and on most days I watched the Buddha, often from only a few yards away, through binoculars, through long camera lenses, through Polaroids . . . the veil lifted between us and I am quite certain that the fish was just as aware of me as I was of him.

The Buddha: what other name to give to a large, rounded, smooth brown leather carp, a creature that appeared so at ease with life, so utterly assured in his world? Why do I call the Buddha 'he'? Surely he is never an 'it'—that would be ridiculous for a creature that was to become virtually a friend. A 'she', perhaps, for a carp of such size must surely be a female but can one really visualise a female Buddha? So, I am quite certain that *he* knew of my puny efforts to catch him.

By the end of the summer I was quite in awe of the fish and perhaps that was part of my undoing. I began to realise that I was confronted by a totally aware creature sensitive to all manner of danger. In a crowded, poorly fed, overfished pool, carp survive by becoming tackle- and bait-wise. Here, in a rich, sparsely stocked, lightly fished water the Buddha was aware of my arrival and my presence because it was something out of tune in his environment: accident did not need to befall this fish for him to react to danger. Simply my presence jarred in his world and the Buddha was so integral a part of it that he could pick up on the discord. In fact this aspect of my relationship with the Buddha did cause me some concern: what right did *I* have to be there at all? It became one of those fishing experiences when I began to feel I was an alien on the water, an intruder, and that fishing was not quite the right thing to do. I began to appreciate why several of the very great carp anglers in the past had given up the sport. To men like Len Bunn, fishing had not lost its appeal as such, but gradually they had come to see it as a disruptive element in nature. However, my interest in the Buddha was so great that I overcame this insidious moral objection to pursuing him.

The Gardener's Lake is phenomenally rich in weed growth of all types, partly because there is a lack of waterfowl as the lake is so close to the house and so the weed is very little cropped. It is also massively enriched from the old septic tanks whose overflow leaches into the lake. This luxuriant growth has probably always been the case, and certainly photographs of the lake pre-war show an area more weed than water. In fact by the end of June, the entire surface of the pool would be encrusted by weed, or very nearly. In the north corner shaded by trees, and over the deepest area close to the small dam, the growth was at its thinnest and I found it possible to pick a few strands of the stuff each day and keep a fair space free. For a long while, I was quite sure that if I troubled to keep the swim reasonably baited and if I fished steadily through enough nights, the Buddha would drift in, feed and give me my chance.

In short, I spent some dozen, wonderful warm nights within sound of the seashore, surrounded by the scufflings of the woodland, on the Gardener's Lake for virtually nothing. What was probably the smallest fish in the lake did come out—pretty and much admired in the first light of dawn but a far cry from the amazing creature that I sought. Ultimately I had to conclude that the Buddha did not use all the lake at night as you might have expected, and nor, in fact, did his lesser companions. Also, just possibly, the clear area of water signalled 'danger' that the fish were keen to avoid.

The obvious answer was to create half-a-dozen small holes, just large enough to take a bait, at various points round the lake. This I did with rake and fork, and made sure that they were all ideally placed over clean sand and close to notable pieces of bank-side cover. I was also careful in choosing the most suitable bottom make-up, and tried to locate depressions where carp had fed

(opposite above) *Two lovely carp hang motionless in the Gardener's Lake*

The Buddha at last! As the fish swam round in the water its colossal back was revealed. I would soon get to know everything about this majestic fish

A typical country sight. A red-legged partridge sits atop the masonry of an outhouse and surveys the parkland scene

in the past. All the holes were large enough to allow the Buddha to enter, turn around at ease, and then tip and feed. This, however, he never did, or certainly at least not when I was in attendance. There was no real reason that I could logically give to the failure of this technique.

But now I come to the most disturbing part of the story. One piece of water was *always* naturally free. It was roughly four feet long by four feet wide and permanently occupied by the fish of my desire. Ever since early June I had never seem him anywhere but in this hole in the weed, and in fact as far as I could tell he was always there. Always. It was, I supposed, his continual presence that kept the weed from encroaching. Even during those nights down by the dam, I had sometimes wandered to the mid-lake and shone the torch over the weed hole . . . and there he would be. The beam would glint off his back or gleam from his stomach in the crystal clear water. Imagine the gloom I would feel the rest of the long night! Each dawn he would be there, and all through the heat of the day following he would be there, and also as dusk crept in, never straying, never leaving. As I have said, many, many hours were spent examining the Buddha in this hole both through binoculars and long camera lenses. Even though I did not catch the fish in this period, I certainly saw enough to leave me pondering. For long periods, quite immobile, hanging back part-exposed, pectorals just occasionally fanning like great coral scallops, the Buddha lay. He was like a giant asleep, but was still aware, alert to my appearance, to the dart of a kingfisher or to the intrusion of a lesser fish—an event that he would sometimes tolerate and sometimes not. When not, he would occasionally explode the hole in an eruption of anger and the whole weed mantle would rock, the coots screech and an eerie silence fall on the lake.

A large part of the day saw the Buddha slightly more active. At these times, finning almost constantly, edging round and round his hole, sometimes tilting, sometimes rocking, the great white lips of the fish would be continually on the move. It was quite a while before I realised what this all meant, and then at last I began to understand. Vast banks of daphnia would frequently drift into the Buddha's hole and he would graze on them hour after hour like a basking whale absorbing food in the high seas. Here was the fundamental explanation I sought to the problem: the Buddha did not need to travel, to bubble, to feed like any normal fish because he never had to leave his own sitting-room—the lake in its fertile generosity brought his food to him. His was a continual breakfast in bed, and it made the catching of him seem at the very least an uphill task.

Pursuing The Buddha

By mid-July my involvement with the Buddha had grown enormously to the point where he had become an obsession with me—a well known danger that may afflict any really dedicated angler from time to time. During these periods any old fish just will not do and your whole being becomes centred upon the One. I suppose to some extent this obsession was allied to the place itself, since

At work clearing the Gardener's Lake of weed. It is a simple matter to tie a large rake head to two pieces of rope, wade out and drag the whole affair back in with a great swathe of weed attached. It is hot, tiring work, but effective—too effective in this case!

for me, the estate was the essential kernel of the valley, a paradise of rolling hills, of deep green oak woods, glimpses of sea and gleaming pools of water.

My passionate interest in the Buddha's lifestyle vied for a long while with my drive as an angler actually to catch him. At long last, the second urge grew too strong to resist and I knew an assault had to be made on the Buddha's hole. I was not too happy about this, and realised that any invasion could affect the fish's well established routine. Furthermore, right from the start I was very unsure if I could get the carp from such a heavily guarded position. There were over twenty yards of extremely thick weed between the Buddha and any bank, and this put the odds firmly in his court. To stand any chance my gear would have to be so powerful that it would be hard to disguise it and fool such a fish in such crystal clear water.

(opposite above) *A distant view of the Buddha in his weed stronghold. His hole is just large enough to accommodate his vast form and he was happy to lie there for weeks—no, months—of the hot summer*

(opposite below) *A close-up of the great fish. The mandarin pectorals are quite visible in the crystal-clear water*

Plan one was the obvious floater attack. For four days I drifted ample selections of different biscuit down the lake, over the whole and within inches of the great fish. That he saw many of these offerings there can be no doubt—some even caught upon his back, and sometimes his dorsal fin would hold up three or four biscuits before he lowered it and they drifted on down with the wind. Never once did I feel at all convinced that the Buddha regarded them with any interest and he certainly did not see them as food; I have always maintained that food-rich estate lake carp tend to ignore floaters and here, it seemed, was a further dramatic example.

Considering the Buddha was totally pre-occupied with very small food items, the next approach was obviously to present particle baits in the hole in the hope he would eventually sip a couple in. Maggots under a controller and on a greased line were drifted four to six inches under the surface past his nose once every hour or so. But again, though my heart beat frantically and I had trouble holding the binoculars steady, he showed no inclination to take the bait. Probably the necessarily heavy line and hook would have dissuaded him even if he had actually taken a fancy to the food. Small red worms, large lobs, wasp grubs procured by the gardener, grasshoppers, moths, pieces of corn, large caddis grubs—nothing made any impact on him whatsoever and the whole approach had therefore to be abandoned.

A more urgent form of attack was called for, and increasingly I found subtlety being shelved. The next move was akin to a blitz; and a large, smelly bait was cast out to lie in the hole in the hope that it would attract the big fish down. I chose a substantial chunk of high-flavoured luncheon meat. The splash of its entry obviously alarmed the Buddha. There was a fountain of water as he splashed and the hole was quiet for fifteen minutes. Then he was back exactly as before. The bait sat untouched for hours and, as I had really expected from the start, it was ignored. This had always been an approach destined to failure.

We were moving now into September and I was becoming a little wild. To give the whole job up seemed the logical course of action, but it was a thing I could not contemplate. Critically at this low ebb my sensibilities were assaulted by one of my more forthright acquaintances, who insisted that my only chance would be to destroy that hole in the weed by simply going out there and raking the whole area free. Don advised against this and so did all my inner voices—and yet, on a blazing afternoon, I found myself half stripped, wading out towards the Buddha, with rope, drag and partner.

In two hours we had taken a great swathe out of the weed bed and the home of the Buddha was gone for the year at least. I sat on the bank at last and looked out at the destruction and at once regretted it deeply. Now it seemed a crazy thing to have done, and as if in confirmation, I was not to see the Buddha again for the rest of the month. I did not deserve to, I realised. You see, I had betrayed what was a kind of trust: that fish had shown so much of itself to me, and this was my manner of repayment.

Water temperatures obviously vary dramatically within any lake or pit. It is an area of research that few men have investigated and certainly on a large, deep pit like this it is obvious that the carp enjoy feeding on a shallow, comparatively warm shelf

The act of desecration itself revealed some of the last things I was to learn concerning the Buddha. The most remarkable was that the water on the shallow shelf by the margin was exceedingly warm, but once you moved off it into 3 to 5 feet of water, the water beneath the weed was cold. This spring water was never revealed to the sun fully and remained at a little over 50°F. In the Buddha's hole, which I examined very carefully before obliterating it, the top 4 to 6 inches of water was close to 70°F, whilst a foot beneath, the temperature fell to the high fifties—still a good few degrees warmer than elsewhere. The great fish obviously made the hole to enjoy the highest possible temperatures, since even the sub-surface zones were kept a little warmer by their exposure to the sun—something that the weed-covered areas did not receive. This temperature band would probably explain why the Buddha was such a visible, surface-loving fish and was so loath to drop any distance down towards the bed of the lake. Since he was at least ten inches from dorsal to ventral, he had presumably been living with his top half warm and his tummy in comparative cold, and this could possibly explain his habit of lifting his back well clear of the water; moving upwards like this just two or three inches could in effect lift his stomach into a mellow warmth that he would find very comforting. This could also explain the frequent and continual pectoral movement as something to do with fanning the warm water along his flanks to the ventral area. Furthermore, the Buddha would also tilt himself from side to side and well up and down rather like we do in a bath, moving our bodies around to get the very best of the warmer water.

Examinations of the weed removed—generally mare's tail, Canadian pondweed and flannel weed—did not reveal it to be especially rich, apart from leeches and small snails. Out there in the lake I found, as I had rather expected, that the real bonanza was in the water-borne life, in the daphnia and water-fleas which were so plentiful that they glittered around us like stardust in the sunlight. Great masses were drifting round the lake, almost always in the top foot of water, and they must have provided the Buddha with an eternal food source that was simplicity itself to harvest. By the nature of this food, any bait larger than a match-head would have been glaringly obvious, out of character, and in all probability shunned.

The summer was less bright after the deed and though I kept up regular visits to the Gardener's Lake, I had no further sightings of the Buddha and guessed that my chances had gone for the summer.

Carp At Hall Lake

Excluding the Buddha, Don had a choice of carp fishing in the valley: there were the Gallows Hill wildies, but also an interesting old stock of mirrors in the Hall Lake, a water so called because it lay at the foot of the formal gardens and had been dug to give scope to the view from the oak-panelled drawing-room. The present owner's father had tried introducing trout, but the water was always too muddied. It was also a heat trap in the summer as it was positioned in a hollow and surrounded by banks of lush rhododendrons.

A slim fish, but beautifully coloured and conditioned

Carp momentarily leave the protection of the lilypads to move out and forage for a short while before returning to sanctuary

Lacking oxygen and that strange vitality a good trout water really needs, one dismal stocking followed another. Browns or rainbows, the species made not one jot of difference, and hardly a single fish ever managed to over-winter.

Determined still to have trout on his estate, the old squire turned his attention to a larger, deeper, clearer pool further away from the house in the wood. He began to put trout in this, with strict instructions to the keeper to keep a good eye on them. There was a path from the village that led to the lake and the squire was only too aware of the skill of the local boys. For the Hall Lake the squire turned his attention to carp, and bought fifty fish to stock it. These fish did well, given the limitations of the water; one that does not have sparkle enough for trout rarely produces the monster carp that fill our dreams. No, the Hall Lake was too shallow, and was lacking those essential ingredients of weed, food supplies and water clarity that make for true monster carp.

The shallowness of the water had its own marked effect on the fish themselves. By shallowness, I mean an average depth of less than one foot but a maximum of two, with four feet of silt beneath. Although this silt allowed the carp to over-winter successfully, it was obviously stifling the entire lake and would in the end spell its doom. In these circumstances, the carp developed impressive length and also high ridged backs that make them look very large in the water (and indeed they *are* large in sane terms) although they do not weigh heavy—their body below the lateral line withers away to virtually nothing, as if their bellies have been shaved away by the constant rubbing on the silt. Certainly, if these fish were pot-bellied in any way, it is hard to imagine how they would cope with such shallow water. Slim as they are, they still spend the summer half-exposed whenever they stray from the deepest depressions or the lilybed to feed in the shallows.

The final element that holds the size of these carp back is their prolific breeding capacity. Shortly after Don's arrival in the valley, the heat began to build up: constant high pressure, long hours of ever more intense sunshine and little breeze led to rocketing temperatures in the shallow water. Then after five days of clear weather, a bank of cloud appeared after sunset one evening. All the wind died away, the stars disappeared and the night became hotter even than the day. Drifting in and out of sleep I was aware of crackling thunder and sheets of lightning that lit up the room, though it did not rain apart from one torrent that came down as brief as water from a spilt pail: the rain hammered at the roof for a minute or perhaps two, and then stopped, leaving the ground moist by dawn. There was then a slight dip in the temperature with a flimsy veil of mist in the lower valleys which cleared at crack of sun-up.

The carp in the Hall Lake had been agitated for the previous two days, swimming in pairs, in threes and in even larger groups. By 7am when Don arrived on that morning, two of these groups met in the lilies, and as their bodies clashed the spray fountained—the spawning had begun, and there followed four hours of mayhem. The lilies were torn up and the branches of the over-hanging alders cracked under the strain of buckling fish. The noise was quite audible 200 yards away where the horses in the field began to whinny uneasily and canter around.

The larger females were carried on the backs of smaller fish, and one particularly handsome linear mirror was thrown two feet in the air; it fell back,

This fish, though a beauty, could weigh at least twice as heavy if it had the large, ugly, distended stomach seen on so many of the imported mirror strains today

On the far side of the lilybeds spawning carp explode into frantic action. All round the silt is stirred up and branches that overhang the water are broken off in the fury of the spawning process

thrashing the water to a muddy foam. The groups of carp merged into orgasmic pyramids twenty or even thirty fish strong. Don watched from the branches of the alder tree quite mesmerised.

By eleven o'clock the activity was slowing down. Here and there carp were lying on their own resting, their mouths clear of the water as they gasped in oxygen. Some were lying on their sides, exhausted. The eels had already emerged from the mud and were beginning to slither hungrily in amongst the lilybeds looking for spawn; then the roach joined in, and in their frenzy for food forgot all their caution. The whole spawning process was thus put in reverse: the carp moved back again into pairs, and then began to patrol again alone; and so the lake was as it had been before.

Time and again throughout the spawning, Don had seen one fish that particularly interested him. She was probably the largest fish in the lake, but more than that, she had a colour about her that he seemed to recognise. She was very pale with dark-coloured fins, and looked exactly like a fish—much smaller then—he had caught twenty years before as a boy. He felt this big female was perhaps one of the orginal stocking, and certainly had a fancy that she was the fish which had excited him so much so long ago. He decided then, as he climbed down from the alder stiff and weary, that try to catch her he must.

Life In The Lilies

The lilybed *is* the Hall Lake and is of great age; it can be seen quite clearly as a fully mature bed in photos of the lake taken *before* the Great War. Probably it has never been cut back and now spreads so huge that it dominates the water, in all possibly a quarter of an acre in extent. It sports white flowers and yellow ones, but it is the pads which are the vital things, huge, waxed coracles large enough to have taken Jeremy Fisher all across the Atlantic to America.

The lilybed is vitally important because of the extreme shallowness of the lake, the usual result of silting and water abstraction. In this case, however, it is so bad that the small fish are only just covered and the largest always have to force themselves along with their backs proud. Without the lilybed, therefore, the carp would be stripped naked; whereas now they have learned how to make the very best use of this lush cover. They lie under it until hunger forces them out, or when they are sure that the coast is clear . . . or until night falls. It is after dusk that life really begins—in the day the lilybed simply serves as a tent, shading the carp from sun, scrutiny and angler's attack. Besides, although a big fish may be hooked in this sanctuary, the chances of landing him simply do not exist: the place is a stronghold.

It is quite possible to wait all day and not see more than half-a-dozen fish,

A carp is lifted bodily out by its attendant males in the middle of the lilybed

and these will almost invariably be smaller ones, unable to contain their hunger and out for a swift forage on the bloodworm that riddle the rich muds. The time, though, is never wasted, and it is a fine, warm place to lie hidden watching the lilypads stir to the bodies beneath. Sometimes they heave to some underwater disagreement, or a head pokes through the screen or a big broad tail waves in the sunlight. Frequently Don would think he saw the fish of memory—he would fancy it to be larger or more distinctly marked than the others, although he could not really be sure from glimpses. He knew he needed to see all the carp and in open water to be able to select the largest— an event that would certainly never come about in daytime.

Therefore one night after The Swallows had closed, he drove up to Frog Hall and walked down the dark path to the lake: and it was a different place now that darkness had released the carp from their prison. The water literally rocked against the banks and the sounds of clooping and slurping reverberated in the still air; great splashes sounded far out and the coots kept up a barrage of alarm. Fascinated, Don walked the banks, and could just see the furrows of fish moving away from him in the dark. After only five minutes all activity had ceased and it was obvious that stealth was as necessary by night as by day; also that a really bright, big moon would be vital for differentiating one fish from another. A blind cast to the wrong fish and a chance of the big one would be gone.

Lilies everywhere, the perfect shade for carp, rudd and tench. Their stems also harbour a certain amount of amount of food which tench in particular find attractive

Beaten at last

A big fish comes into view

   The full moon rose on the fifteenth and it was a startlingly clear night with temperatures dropping rapidly. Even a hundred yards away, Don could hear the Hall Lake chattering with activity; he crept to the massive, centrally placed oak tree and blended his form with the great trunk. For a full hour he did nothing but watch: fish after fish he studied, often through binoculars that intensified the light and brought each fish to his fingertips. The scale was confusing, however, and time and again he was sure he had located the biggest fish, only to see a still larger one on the outskirts of his vision. Even without the field glasses, he found it impossible to gauge the size of anything accurately. Then by the lilies one fish surfaced that was massive: it made its way close to the oak roots where it emerged again, all of 6lb!

   By 2am mist was swirling in off the land and the lake was 'smoking' in the fast-cooling air. Carp activity had perceptibly decreased and Don realised that time was no longer on his side. For twenty minutes past he had been watching a fish with intent: sometimes it looked very long and broad, at others just an average fish—but now circumstances dictated action. The rod, naturally, was ready made up, a large lobworm on the hook . . . weight enough itself for the five-yard cast. Through the binoculars, the skull of the fish was still plain enough even through the mist, and with his first swing, the lobworm landed just twelve inches in front of it.

(opposite above) *A float lies on the fringe of the lilies and a fish is just beginning to bubble close to it*

(opposite below) *A fish makes a lightning forage from the mantle of the protective lilypads. These raids are swift and full of trepidation. Even a bird swooping down low will send fish surging back to cover*

The influence of the moon upon fish behaviour is an enthralling one. It is true to say that some of the most famous continental carp anglers will only fish during the full and the new moon phases. It is well known that the moon not only influences the tides but also all human and animal behaviour, and it does seem possible that it can also affect fish feed patterns as well. One problem with fishing during the full moon is that frequently the nights are particularly cold. Perhaps it is better to sacrifice the light and gain some warmth and fish during those periods of a new moon

In the crinkling light of the spreading eddies it was hard to see anything exactly, but soon line was peeling off the spool and Don struck into a decent fish. Predictably it made straight for the lilybed, and the only crisis of the short battle was played out on it fringe. Thereafter it was simply a matter of pulling the fish those final feet through inches of water over four feet of mud. The carp would not come to Don, and Don had to wade to it. It lay on its side in the moonlight: 24in, perhaps 25in long, it was plainly not *the* fish, and so it was unhooked where it lay. Cold now and wet from the thighs down, the night was over for Don, so he tackled down and drove home.

In August, I took to visiting the Hall Lake myself over a period of a few days when the cloud cover was dense and there was a hint of drizzle now and again on the breeze. Actually it was mist rather than true cloud, and inland skies

The tragic sight of a badger hit by a car during the night. Fortunately the valley has two major setts, both stretching to virtually an acre and perhaps housing up to fifteen or twenty mature creatures. Between these two major settlements there are also a number of smaller satellite setts, each holding a small family of animals

The water at Hall Lake is so shallow that a fish need not be netted but simply beached on the mud banks

remained a flawless blue, but it did have the effect of luring fish out of the lilies during the daytime. I was quick to spot a much larger fish than most. Session after session he would bubble and forage disdainfully round my bait and as I got to know him, I felt he got to know me even better, and that my chances were next to nil.

One morning I strolled to the lake and there the fish was as usual, feeding in his usual sort of way. I put on a quite normal lobworm—a bait I had tried several times—and swung it into his path. He crept up to it, sneered at it with his usual contempt—and took it on the spot! Why this fish had deserted his normal caution I will never know, but perhaps I now do understand that even the wiliest fish can made a mistake if you persevere long enough. Whatever, the carp was a remarkable creature, long and lean with fins the size of propellers. I was sad that Don was not with me, but took the best photographs I could, then returned the fish quickly to the water.

A beaten fish comes to the net

The big fish begins to bubble round the bait. Its activity is continuous and it edges closer and closer to the danger zone

A powerhouse of a fish. Look at the size of that shovel tail

VALLEY RIVER

Running Waters

An examination of the map shows that a trickle of water leaves the Gallows Hill pool and flows by a series of ditches through woods and field to the Rectory stream. This brook runs a further mile before entering the upper reaches of the river proper. Such is the route, probably, that the occasional otter uses when he visits the pool for a feast of carp. This is the waterway the few large eels followed years before, as elvers then, nosing their way from the sea in search of a freshwater home.

The Rectory stream is a very secretive waterway, only a foot or so deep, eight feet wide perhaps and twisting almost its entire course through woodland. Despite the heavy autumn leaf fall of oak, birch and alder, the stream keeps itself clear with its very lively current, and for the whole of its length the bottom is alternating sand and gravel. Every large stone hides a crawfish, a loach or a gudgeon and the whole stream teems with very small brown trout although these rarely reach more than a couple of ounces before being taken by an otter or one of the herons that understandably haunt the place.

The wood is full of shadows and in the village has a reputation for spirits. Indeed it is only when the stream runs out of the wood at last and crosses a common for a quarter of a mile that it is fished at all by the local boys. Even a gudgeon here is a triumph—but the promise of trout in plenty cannot lure them further upstream into the woodland.

Crossing the common, the Rectory stream enters the river at the tail of the millpool. Over the years, a few trout with ambition have left this nursery stream for the larger water where the food choice will be greater and the chances of survival higher. Certainly from time to time in the past very large trout indeed have been recorded, caught—or more often seen—chasing dace and small roach in the shallows, or shearing through the minnow shoals with jaws snapping audibly above the roar of the water. When Don and I were boys a massive creature of 14lb was caught upon a frog and hand line and then hung up outside The Swallows porch for two days. I remember how we gawped, and went back again and again to gawp even further. The men inside would laugh through the windows and say that one day when we were grown up, we too would catch a fish to such proportions. In the end, I remember, the cats got at it and what was left was taken down and fed to the pigs. In those days there was such plenitude in the river that even this did not seem a shame, and no one doubted bigger trout could and would be caught in the future.

Of course, the villagers were not to know that changes would come to the valley and affect the river. Indeed, the decline in the numbers and sizes of trout

Even though it is high summer and no rain of any significance has fallen for months, the stream still flows with guts and spirit

A place of spirits . . .

(opposite) *The Rectory stream twists through its woodland, home to small trout, to crayfish, roach and bullheads*

has hardly been constant, and as late as 1980 I saw one beautiful seven pounder taken on a small dace. Even now the river is not done, and in the spring just past I did actually see a large trout again, surging and leaping after the fry shoals. My conservative estimate had been 6lb, but my heart had whispered 8lb. But then, it has always been hard to guess the weight of these fish. Big river trout do not hold station in the currents like normal-size ones, where they can be viewed at leisure: their habit is to hide behind boulders, in deeper clefts or in undercuts until the light is right for an attack, generally in the half- or quarter-gloom of dawn or dusk. Then the big spotted predator will hammer out into the fry shoals like a piscine sledgehammer. This is what I had recently witnessed, and the speed of the fish was such that I could not swear at all to its size. Still, his presence alone had excited and inspired me to investigate further.

Looking at the river that morning I began to wonder about my despair concerning its well-being, and Don himself remarked that he had expected to notice more obvious signs of decay. From this first millpool the course of the river is comparatively short, the length of the valley in fact, around ten miles. Then, it opens out to meet the sea. Though a small river and despite all the demands made upon it, the flow remains quite lively due, largely, to the effect of the numerous springs along its course. It is these springs that are also responsible for the crystal clarity of the water, which for me is one of the major delights of the river: apart from storms and heavy winter deluges, the water is a window to the world beneath its surface. If the fish there are hard to catch, and they are, then they are also easy to observe, and the joy of any capture is really and truly enhanced.

Slightly beneath the millpool runs a footbridge over the river, and here we found the boy Chamberlain fishing for eels. The water under the footbridge is deep and strewn with rubble, generally old masonry that has fallen in through many years. Some decent eels have always been found living there, whilst lesser fish have stopped over during their journeys around the valley. Chamberlain is nearly always on the river whether he should be at school or not, and it is always wise to ask what he has seen. At it was, he had an eel of perhaps 2lb dangling from the bars of his bicycle, already decapitated and ready for tea. It is never any use explaining to him the glories of the eel's lifecycle and the wondrous tale of its wanderings from sea to freshwater and back again. Chamberlain will simply explain how all his folks have taken eels from that bridge and pedalled them to the cottage and eaten them at the rough pine table. This is how Chamerlains have lived for centuries—and there's obviously no changing this latest one.

However, what neither of us missed was Chamberlain's bait. When he reeled in we saw a chunk of roach on his hook. The piece was around an inch square, and still sported the dead fish's dorsal fin. Looking around us we saw more cubes of fish lying diced in a bait box. We tipped them out onto the verge and set about a grizzly jigsaw puzzle. There were perhaps a score or even more of bits and pieces—a head here, a tail, a pelvic fin, a chest—in the end the sad

The stream meanders across the common where the village boys learn their fishing (and later their courting)

Two superb roach from the past, fish of probably eight or ten years of age, grown large on the rich diet of shrimps and snails that are found in alkaline waters. The depth of the bottom fish is particularly impressive with its bullish shoulders and stocky physique, and suggests real power and growth ability

figure lay before us in the grass. We measured it. Fifteen inches long. There was no doubt about it—it was a true roach, and the pieces available to us, dried out and blood-stained as they were, still weighed 2lb 2oz.

The Chamberlains' precious past now be blowed! *No more*, we told this one, when dace of an ounce or so were to be had nearly as easily as lobworms from the vegetable patch, from the church lawns or from the farmyard tip. We made such a row about it all that the poor lad was thoroughly alarmed, and was quick to tell us where the shoal had been just three hours before. You needn't doubt we hurried off to look.

(opposite) *The river still has a lush growth of some of the best waterweed. Here great beds of ranunculus are seen waving in the gentle current*

Roach And The Wheel Of Nature

Some men have their grouse moors, some their deer forests, others their salmon pools: I have my roach river, and as Don and I hurried off downstream that day, I knew there could never have been a lovelier one. Red brick bridges, riverside cottages, all lush greens, yellow lilies—and above all, in little pockets, the gold and crimson of roach themselves. It was easy to forget my laments for the valley as the sun broke through and glinted on fish after fish and their dazzling scarlet banner fins. Indeed, I had happily to admit that, in spite of so many very real pressures, the roach were flooding back. In part I was surprised—but then, the valley roach had seen bleak times before.

Sixty years ago, if local lore is to be believed, the river's roach all but disappeared. The deep pool, the cabbage-fringed runs and shaded eddies were devoid of big fish; the shallows held no fingerlings. There was a slight lament, but nothing really could be blamed. The river looked as it had done for

Portrait of the roach river towards the end of the twentieth century. The banks are neat and the river's course is almost ruler-straight, apart from the occasional kink left by the dredger. Here, however, at least willows have been planted to break the wind and they provide some sort of shade from the sun. Their presence also means that the bank will not be dredged again in the future and already the reedbeds are beginning to spread, providing shelter for fry and fingerlings and food for roach of all sizes

generations, and disease was generally held to be the cause of the decline; there
was no firm evidence whatsoever. A few men remarked on the phenomenon
and noticed how bare the river appeared then without its most central species.
What roach remained had a hard time of it through World War II. Food was,
of course, in very short supply, and by 1945 and 1946 not only were the roach
desperately few, but dace and pike had been so heavily thinned out by the
farmhands that few returning servicemen troubled to fish the waters of their
boyhood. It was all very sad, but after the events of six war years hardly an
abscess on the affairs of men.

Through the 1950s the river lay fallow and disregarded. Only around 1959
did news filter through the villages that roach were back, and back with a
vengeance. Evenings, weekends and holidays, and the fishermen were there.
The catches were immense. Men called it all a miracle and agreed that the
fishing was better than it had been in the old days. 'Leave it to Mother Nature
to get things right,' said some. And just like the old days it was, with men
teaching boys and bicycles leaning against the bridge. Fishermen were
skipping church and the riverside was again a busy place on any summer
evening.

Sadly, and perhaps inevitably, this heyday was not to last long: after a few
years, the vast roach shoals were devastated by the disease columnaris that

*Columnaris in close-up. The ghastly red, bubbling sores spread over the flanks of the
fish and eventually cause disfigurement and very often death*

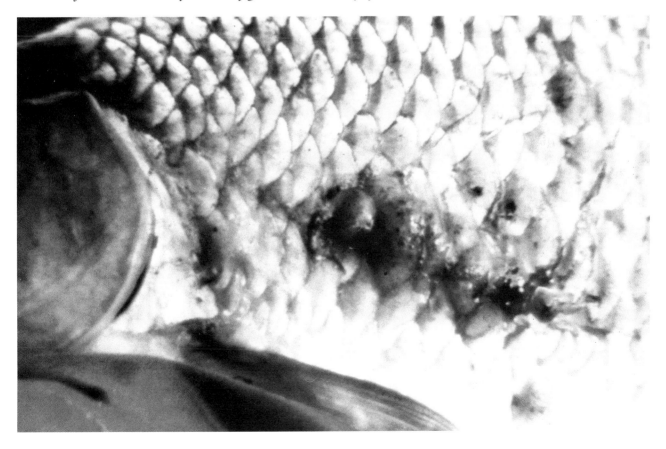

A beautifully conditioned summer dace lies amidst the flowers of the season. Even though a dace is a small fish it is still very quick to differentiate between the free offering and the hooked bait

cripples, disfigures and kills. Thousands of roach bearing deep sores and lesions died, and once more it was felt that roach were fish of the past. Not so. The numbers of fish before the outbreak had been underestimated, and also a percentage of roach actually managed to overcome the disease and survive. True, they were sad and scarred creatures to behold but they lived on, often for twenty more years.

The early 1970s then were far from a disappointment, and many said that the stocks of big fish had never been higher. Superb roach between 13 and 15 inches long were common and the giants of 16 to 18 inches were not unknown. Fabulous fish, fabulous days; but by 1978 doomed to decline.

For the next decade, the roach stocks were particularly low—old men said at least as bad as the 1930s—and now with the pressures of pollution and abstraction we saw no road back. In fact the roach that did remain were often huge, anything between 16 and a colossal 19 inches long. But they were few, desperately few in number. It seemed that there was not the springboard of mature fish to produce fry enough for a comeback, so a continued inexorable decline seemed inevitable. For the anglers, half-a-dozen roach a season was good: in the end, even a single fish was considered fair when half the river could be walked and not a roach would be seen on even the best of spotting days. This had to be the end.

(opposite) *One of the favourite roach swims of all is under this massive willow tree that provides a little extra depth and a great deal of cover from the hot sun*

Then, slowly at first, evidence of new fish began to emerge. A word here, a sighting there, and even a catch of 8oz roach was reported. In 1988, small mint-fresh roach were seen in just a handful of places. Through 1989 the shoals spread and quite suddenly, as the last decade of the 20th century began, the roach were back. It was Nature's miracle to keep the wheel turning. Perhaps a succession of warm summers and mild winters worked the magic. Perhaps, like perch, roach simply operate over decade-long cycles and the river will again see decline in ten, fifteen or twenty years and men will again be in despair. Nevertheless, if we continue to treat our rivers as mindlessly as we do now, there must still come a final reckoning. Mankind cannot for ever rely on the power of Nature to heal and restore the vein of life we seem intent on severing.

The boy Chamberlain was to be believed, and at last Don and I found ourselves staring at a large shoal of huge roach. It was a sight I had never expected to enjoy again. Being there, with Don, in front of such fish was re-living a bygone period of my life. For minutes we watched in silence, in our own world of thoughts. I have to describe how roach light up the water, especially with the sun on them as it was then. Their old country name 'red fin' seems so appropriate and such an apt reminder of what our rivers once were— all clear, bright places before *we* had learned how to despoil and to destroy.

Chamberlain's directions had allowed us to approach the shoal unobserved and the fish remained calm, high in the water, in perfect order. A panicked shoal moves constantly, often patrolling a twenty- to thirty-yard stretch in nervy agitation, whilst individual members jostle for prime positions. We counted just over twenty-five fish. I, personally, was afraid to guess the size of the largest; a fish or two would just have to be caught to establish some sort of scale, some comparisons. There were three fish, though, that I simply must mention here, for the sight of them never left my head that summer long. Two were quite enormous: whatever angle of their massive bodies they presented, they never looked less than 3lb; and the third roach—well, I had simply never, ever seen its like before. When we did at last talk, Don said it must be a chub. But it wasn't. It was the roach of all my dreams, the pinnacle of my newly revived roach river.

First Successes

The last part of our journey was along the Roman causeway that served the mill, and we followed it up to the fine old barns and the bridge where the millpool thundered. It was a fine evening in early June so there was plenty of light about, the water glowed silver under the rising moon and the vapour of the millrace was a cooling influence on what was to become a very hot night.

Indeed, even in these early days there was every indication that the summer would become a hot one.

The river was very active: dace were busy in the shallows, minnows flickered in the margins and small trout plopped consistently after moths in the full flow. We had a single fly rod with us and we took it in turns to flick a large, white floating artificial into the current. The fishing was not purist but it was pleasant, and we soon had two trout of ten inches or so that would make a good change for supper. There were no signs of any big fish, but Don was suitably enough impressed to get up long before dawn the following day and be ready at first light for another session. This is what he later reported.

After only a few minutes, shoals of small fish began to shower the tail of the weir. The activity was continual and he worked his way through the tall wet grasses to get closer to the area. There was by now sufficient light to show a large dark shape moving quickly here and there under the surface; in fact so high in the water did it travel that often its fin and even its back broke clear. The fish was a brown trout, a monster for such a small stream.

Don was so enthralled by the sight of this giant at its breakfast that his tackle remained unused against the mill wall. Quite suddenly the fish disappeared, the water was quiet and the small dace began to flip merrily about without anxiety once more. Excited as he was, Don had been able to make some accurate observations on the feeding trout. It had been active for just over fifteen minutes and had not fed consistently but had taken three small breaks of around a minute each. These, almost certainly, were the occasions when a dace had been caught and the trout went into deeper water to swallow it. Many of the big trout's strikes were abortive—probably three or perhaps four were successful out of an estimated total of twenty. It is fortunate for the predator that dace shoal so thickly, or these percentages would be down even further. Perhaps it is surprising that the big brown bothered with dace at all, for surely he would have been better served by hunting the furtive bullheads or crawfish or loach. A trout is not a born predator in the way of pike or perch: the large cannibal trout is in some ways something of a freak of Nature and has to work hard to overcome the limitations of its hunting abilities.

The whole episode excited Don greatly, and he spent some time catching small dace and putting them in a trap ready for a serious attempt on the fish. Thus the following morning he set out a second time with a light carp rod, 8lb line and a size 6 hook already attached. This time he had to wait far longer for action—in fact the day was becoming quite bright and sunny before the big fish appeared on the shallows again.

Immediately Don hooked a 3in dace through the lips and cast it to the tail of the pool. He could see the little fish twisting in the shallow water, and twice the big trout closed on it but powered past without taking. The third time, though, was the last: the black shadow engulfed the silver dace and the line ran out against the flow towards the deeper water.

Everything happened so quickly that Don hardly knew how to react or how long to give the taking fish. Still, the trout looked large and the bait was small, so he struck as soon as the line stopped being taken. The fight was not particularly exciting as the fish kept deep, apart from two soaring leaps that threatened to throw the hooked dace skywards. On the bank, however, the trout was majestic: 8lb 4oz, spots as big as blackberries, with a finely formed head and body, teeth as sharp as those of a pike, and fins perfect down to the last ray. Don looked long and hard at the creature before sliding it back into the oxygen-filled water, and then walking home to his cottage a happy man.

The big trout is held to recover in the water. This may take quite a while, for a trout, far more than most coarse fish, is very susceptible to the stress of capture. The fish is held in the tail of the weir, pointing upstream, so that the water can rush through its mouth and gills and feed it valuable oxygen

The Upper River Monsters

With me lost to the Buddha, Don had a clear run at the big roach of the upper river, and the occasion of his first success is well worth recounting. After that first day when we had found the shoal, he had experienced great difficulty locating it again. Four miles of river can easily absorb twenty or thirty fish, and conditions for fish-spotting must be perfect. Unfortunately, for some days, Don was dogged by the worst possible combination of chop on the water and lack of bright sunlight. The breeze was strong and constantly upriver, and this distorted vision a couple of feet down. Good light is also vital and the wind blew in a thin cloud that made the sun very hazy. Visibility was further

(opposite above) *The trout lies beaten at last. Notice the fish's rugged jaws now adapted to a diet of fingerlings and fry*

(opposite below) *The big trout goes back into the glistening water, and is held against the current until the gills begin to beat*

restricted and the bends and pools over 5 or 6ft deep remained a mystery. These, of course, were the very places that big roach were likely to be during the daylight hours as they waited to move on at dusk and begin feeding in earnest.

On the day in question, the early hours had come in rather cold and the wind had been such a stiff one that Don had very nearly stayed in late. However, by first light the wind had very nearly died away, and what remained was easily absorbed by the poplars and kept off the river which now ran placid as a mill pond. In these conditions, Don felt quite confident that a roach might roll and betray its companions. When a roach does roll it is often not with the clear sight of red fins that old authors love to describe, as though the whole boil is covered crimson. It is more an impression of silver and red than anything specific, just the instant knowledge that the fish are there.

But there was nothing, not all the way down to the footbridge by the church. Pool after pool he investigated, peering over the reeds, scanning the deeper velvety water. It was a period of intense concentration, full of imaginings and hopes, but not until the run of the very slight bend did he see, six feet down, the glow and pattern of red fins he was seeking.

Eventually the sun came up fully and Don could see every fish in the shoal before him—it was an awe-inspiring moment. Even though every one was a splendid fish, he could still recognise the three largest with ease. They stood out head and shoulders from the rest, and the largest of all even dwarfed the other two. In short, he was stunned by the size of this monster—in fact neither of us had ever had anything to compare it with in all our fishing experience. If we were right, that the general run of fish weighed between 2 and $2\frac{1}{4}$lb, then this, the leader, could easily have weighed double that. Seeing and believing are two quite distinct things and without physical proof, even to mention the existence of a possible $4\frac{1}{2}$lb roach is to strain credibility. Nevertheless, it is quite possible that an old but well conditioned fish in a massively rich environment where very little competition exists could grow to such a size. We know that Wessex rivers can produce roach of over 4lb and here conditions were at least as favourable. Yet I have to admit that all discussion of this huge fish is hypothetical: perhaps his depth was not as great as we guessed, maybe it had that occasional 'hollowness' that reduces the weight of a fish considerably, perhaps it was a hybrid—bar having the fish on the bank and observing it minutely there was always this possibility. All I can say is, that here was a fish Don and I would gladly have died for!

Quite definitely the shoal sensed Don's presence no matter how quiet he tried to be. Obviously he kept his shadow well away from the fish and stalked them using every scrap of cover available to him, but still they remained nervy and restless, moving up and down the river for twenty or thirty yards but always coming back to this same area just on the bend. To Don, there seemed nothing to recommend it. The river here was shallow, bare of cover apart from silkweed, and the only attraction possible could be the patches of sand that lay here and there amongst the green strands. One area, about a yard long toward the far side of the river, was particularly favoured and roach seemed to hang there longer than usual. They also crossed it low down in the water as though willing to browse on any food that they might find there.

A beautiful stretch of roach river. The water clarity can easily be seen from the photograph and the large banks of weed give perfect cover for a roach shoal. Trees also give protection as do the continual encroaching reedbeds. The presence of swans is also a good sign, indicating there is an abundance of water-weed which again provides oxygen, shade and food for the fish

Don began to feed in flake, tiny pieces here and there, now and again, and though the roach would sometimes drift towards them they never took a single mouthful. Indeed, after a couple of hours and when some forty or fifty offerings had been made, the fish became decidedly uneasy and even began to flee from the white pieces as they descended. Maggots were treated no better and Don rested the area as it seemed that the fish were on the point of breaking up altogether. He left the woodland belt and went on to the field stretch of the river where he amused himself watching the swans bullying for territory and kicking the river into uproar.

He was quite sure that his choice of bait had been correct. Even virgin roach seemed quite happy to accept bread as food upon very first sighting. Something about the colour, texture and smell of bread makes it instantly attractive to them and Don had no hesitation in using it on these fish. He did wonder briefly about trying a natural bait, a worm perhaps or a snail, but all previous experience told him to stick out with bread. He felt sure that the reluctance of the fish to feed was not so much the bait itself but more to do with the finicky mood of the shoal. Probably the day was too bright, or the fish had sensed his presence. His confidence remained high.

An hour later, the roach were still on the bend and they had settled down considerably, simply nosing the current again and occasionally rolling over on to their sides with a dull gleam. It was now late morning and the heat was intense. Choosing a moment when there were no roach over the piece of sand, Don introduced a handful of mashed flake, intending it to settle all the way along it. Then he retired to the field stretch again, and wandered along it looking for dace. The bread was still visible on the sand after half-an-hour, but forty-five minutes after that it had all been mopped up, although the depth there was a mere two feet so swans could have eaten it or even a passing shoal of dace. Choosing his moment, more flake went out and Don set himself to watch. As before, the shoal grew uneasy and again he had to vacate the bank. The heat was now quite intense and this decided him on a pint at The Swallows; upon his return, rather later than expected, the roach were there and the bread was not.

Twice more this routine repeated itself, and it was late afternoon when the fifth deposit of bread was made. Don sat right back now in the reeds some four yards from the streak of white flake quite visible in the water and, thoroughly hidden, he waited. It was a world of total peace and he was completely camouflaged. A vole played around a rod length from him; villagers used the bridge sixty yards beneath and never even suspected his presence. His tackle was made up now that he sensed the time was ripe. His rod was 13ft long, light and delicate but with the power to hustle a heavy fish from weed and the other shoal members. The line was 3lb breaking strain straight through to a size 10 hook. He used an ancient peacock quill float, set 2ft over depth so that it would ride the slow current. There could not be better bite indication than this and he felt his hopes begin to soar.

Minutes, an hour, even longer, and shadows at last over the bread, gleams of red and gold and puffs of flake disturbed and disappearing. At last a cast could be made. It had to be a long one and well past the sand bar (a roach that saw the flake drop bolted from it), and then it was edged carefully back into position on the tail end of the clear area. For twenty minutes Don stared at the bait, never daring to switch his gaze. From time to time the white was obscured by a passing form and his hand tightened over the reel. Then a long dark shape appeared behind the flake: the two seemed to merge. The float tremored, stood up and dipped away, and that was it. A great head and pair of shoulders wallowed over the net cord and the roach lay on the reeds. It was a monster. The time was 6pm, and Don had been on the river thirteen hours for that one superb roach. In all, it represented some six days of continual effort and would never have been caught by the casual angler.

The roach itself was a monument to the past. In patches the scales had been displaced by diseases long since thrown off, and the fish was also scarred in five places—one a deep healed wound that must have been the slash of a pike, an otter or a mink. This old roach must have been one of the few to produce spawn in the darkest days of the early 1980s, an effort that resulted in the big fresh fish of the 1990s. It deserved all respect, was soon returned to the river where it melted into the shadows and presumably rejoined the shoal that had broken up the very moment the hook went in and it had made its single, desperate, powerful lunge for safety.

One of the new fresh fish coming to the valley. This is only an eight-or-ten-ounce roach, but shows all the signs of being a magnificent fish in the future

A very big roach lies on a bed of lilypads. This fish is probably at least twelve years old and could well be as much as thirty. Below and behind its dorsal fin are the remains of columnaris scars. Scattered here and there on its flanks are small outbreaks of blackspot, fortunately not a fatal disease. Directly above the fish's pectoral fin and behind its gill flap is an old wound, probably a heron stab mark. Certainly it is a wonder this fish is still alive

———— Attempt On The Tidal River ————

'It's stupid even to consider trying for it, one big fish from a mile or more of thin clear water! But I've been thinking over the options. I can sit it out, well hidden, in a likely place with a decent bait and keep quiet for a day or two. Problems? The river is shallow and the bait will be attacked by every passing waterfowl. Probably the fish only travels when it feels threatened and it could be days before it appears—and then it spooks. Or it ignores the bait or I miss the bite.

'Or I can stalk it. I can locate it and watch it and make sure it settles. Then I can set up as close as possible and wait—at least then I'll know I'm in the right area. I can spend the night and see where it is at dawn, always presuming of course I haven't caught it during the darkness.' There was a long silence. 'Well, I'm going to give it a go.'

He found the fish at his first attempt. The very bright setting sun was perfect for spotting and having very, very, carefully covered half a mile Don came across it a couple of yards from the bank. He withdrew instantly and hid behind nettles to watch it. There was no doubt it was a great fish of fabulous beauty. Once again the salt had had a dramatic effect—its scales were a white silver, its fins the acutest red. It was a fish Don wanted greatly. He drew back into the field and settled in seventy yards upriver on a deeper bend. He put out some bait and two rods and settled back. It was 8pm.

Tackle was simple. His rod was a light 11ft Avon design with a test curve of just over the pound. Line to the size 8 hook was 3lb breaking strain and a 2 swan shot leger link provided the weight to cast and to hold the current. He chose to use an isotope butt indicator that would be heavy enough for the sluggish river and presents little resistance to a taking fish. Bait, as is usual with roach, was bread. He believed it would be plainly visible to the roach if the big fish should pass close during the night. For that same reason he used a large piece of flake on the bigger than average hook: he did not want the fish to be there and to leave without seeing it at all.

5am: it was light enough almost to see the bottom of the river. Don got up from his chair and scanned the water four hundred yards downstream and four hundred yards upstream, but there was no sign of the great roach. He went home for breakfast.

Don fished here and there for the next few days but it was becoming increasingly obvious to him that the fish would need to be seen and fished for specifically. There was just too much water for any other method to be possible. This said, the fish would still need to be seen at its optimum feeding time, either first or last light, and preferably the former. Mind made up, Don prepared again.

In the grey light of a pewter dawn he settled himself on the highest point, a steep bank, from where he could see two hundred yards upriver and almost the same distance down. He was hoping for a bow wave or a roll, or anything that would give him a clue as to the fish's whereabouts. Soon it was light enough to see in the water—an eel was feeding hard, whiplashing into the silt, mouth working as minute bloodworms were thrown up and exposed; a small perch appeared from nowhere. He was happy to see that the species lived on there, but sad when he remembered what a fine perch stretch the tidal reaches had been, twenty-five years ago. The infamous perch disease had struck in the late 1960s, and all one springtime the river had been littered with the ulcerated corpses of fish weighing up to nearly 4lb. In their prime they had been very beautiful fish. The saline content of the water had given added lustre to their scales and deep barred patterns, and rich feeding on shrimps and sand eels had produced massive humps around their shoulders. The agony of seeing those fish in death would never be forgotten, and perhaps that small perch was a herald of a species reborn.

In the estuary the tide was well up, holding the river back so slack that it was like a long narrow pond. He had thrown in some crusts an hour before and

It is a shame that very often the chub get in the way of the roach angler or the barbel man, for the species is a worthy opponent and has a bold brassy beauty all of its own. The chub of the tidal reach is a typical fish in as much as it is a pioneer to a new stretch of water. The lack of food competition has obviously helped its growth for very often these pioneer fish are over five pounds in weight. Once a regular stock of fish appears and breeding becomes frequent and populations rise, the size of individual specimens begins to drop quickly. The tidal reach river must have suited the chub perfectly; being omnivorous it would have been able to make use of all manner of food sources, from runs of shrimp and elver to the hordes of sticklebacks that frequent such brackish places

(above) *Too beautiful to be despised, but a disappointment nonetheless*

(opposite) *The owl, still active before dawn, settles by a birch tree to investigate the rummaging of a mouse*

they had only made their way fifty yards downstream; now they were being picked off by a busy coot and a group of terns that had wheeled in from the saltmarsh.

Don realised that he was falling asleep. The chances of the roach he reckoned were now zero, and he decided he might as well laze for a while in this lovely place. He set up his old Optonic and threw out two handfuls of bread into the deeper run opposite a thick reedbed. He switched on the bite indicator, cast out and sat back, soon finding himself drawn irresistibly into sleep. It was just 6am by the church clock.

Two hours later, the alarm gave two short calls and Don sat up, instantly alert. The bobbin had moved, but that could have been wind or weed and he was not too concerned. He watched the line sag to the water and was on the point of reeling in and going home for breakfast when it sprang tight. His hand was on the rod just as the Optonic sounded.

As soon as he hooked the fish he was sure that this was the one he wanted. It made three slow, sullen runs and then gave up, coming into the net right on the glare of the sun's reflection. The handle bent, and though there was some weed around the fish, Don was certain that this was the big one—it just *had* to be. He staggered with it into the meadow, lay it down, then cursed and sat back. He unhooked it and slipped it back into the river without even weighing it.

The fish was a chub.

Even the fact that it was the first that anybody had seen in the river before failed to pacify him.

The Dewatering Summer

By late summer there had been no appreciable rain for many, many weeks; the spring had been cold and uncommonly dry and now a beating sun and warm winds dried the valley like a prune. Everything began to suffer. The effects on a particular small colony of newts that lived up a drainage dyke behind some large white willows were disastrous: their dyke became a pool which became a puddle which finally became nothing at all, and the little amphibians were either dried like parchment or picked over by the herons—frogs on the move for moisture, rudd in shrinking ponds, the herons had them all. Nothing however, suffered more than the eel in this time, the poor old eel whose shape and slimy body and cold, bleak yellow eyes have turned every hand in Nature against it. There was a heron working the shrinking dyke. He stabbed down and a foot-long eel writhed, caught across the pectorals. Round and round the heron's throat the eel coiled itself, twisting right over the bird's head. The heron swallowed the fish half-way down its scrawny throat but the still-wriggling form, pulling the feathered skin this way and that, was still too powerful. The heron coughed it up and walked to the dyke to take in water; it then returned to its task until inevitably the eel was lost to the world.

The heron flew off, almost certainly to join his cronies on the dead tree above Gallows Hill pond. The grey-coated gentlemen had taken to assembling

The tragic sight of an old pond now dried out. After only a year the bottom lining of these ponds cracks irreparably and if rain should fall it simply seeps away through the fissures and is lost. Apart from a complete relining, a pond in this state is lost for ever

There is hardly water enough to cover the hooves of the animals and a fish lies dead, asphyxiated in less than an inch of water

A wild carp lies on the mud, badly attacked by herons and barely alive. Its death is a lingering one as the sun begins to dry it to parchment

there day after day around the dying pool, like so many undertakers, whilst the water continued to shrink, pea-green and thick as soup. It was a blind life for the carp in there, a world of sense and touch only, fish that only months before had been entombed in ice and were now baked in heat and stalked constantly by the heron troop and the occasional passing otter. Almost every fish had wounds, open or sealed along its back or flanks where the heron's beak had stabbed but been unable to hold on to the wiry powerful form.

And then one morning we, too, wandered to Gallows Hill, for the first time in three weeks perhaps. It was a grey day, but with mist rather than cloud and it would not rain; the crops were parched, the meadows were turning brown, volatile as tinder—and Gallows Hill had all but gone, though it took us a while to realise it. The skim of water, an inch deep across the mud, moved in the wind and for a moment fooled us. Then we saw a dead carp lying on the silt almost totally above the waterline, and the terrible truth dawned upon us. The margins were littered with dead fish, eyes picked clean, some gnawed by the vermin of the woodland. We collected and buried thirty, then realised that we

(opposite) *The saddest sight. Wild carp lie dead on the side of Gallows Hill, trampled by the drinking cattle*

were wasting our time on the corpses and that it was those still alive that had to be dealt with most urgently.

For a whole day, Don and I waded with nets and dustbins trying to catch the wild carp that survived. It was a hot, frustrating, muddy, backbreaking business; wading through the mud of centuries, often above the waistline, is a killer—the legs ache, and as the water creeps into the boots, the cramps start. Carp that we were trying to save would squirm off our net rims and leap out of the buckets and do anything but let themselves be rescued. Like eels, they would push themselves over the mud whilst we floundered, hopelessly outdistanced, in pursuit. How their desperately working gills sucked in enough oxygen from the filthy water I will never know. Our boots kept knocking against solid objects—old posts, bricks, debris, we thought, but no: they were carp, dead and rotting in the silt. By the end of the day we had rescued forty fish and placed them all in small ponds around the valley from where they could be retrieved if and when the time came.

The owner of the water was alerted and the phone wires buzzed. At dawn the following day, mechanical diggers appeared and for four days the silt was gouged out bucket by bucket. A pump was sunk at the northern end of the pond and poured in thousands of gallons of pure cool spring water each hour; near it the surviving wildies gathered, the fresh oxygen coursing through their bodies. It was a round-the-clock operation. The pump had to be refuelled around midnight, and at approximately 3am as daybreak approached, one of us had to be by its outflow to protect those vulnerable carp from the ever-increasing heronry. Each sun-up, the digger drivers would reappear once more and the work would start again to bring Gallows Hill back to life.

The operation was expensive, unprecedented and successful. No more fish

Work begins. The bold first step was to clear away the silt and the mud at the top of the pool, hoping to uncover some hidden springs. This worked to some extent as can be seen from the large standing puddles around the Land-Rover, but the inflow of new water was not fast enough to save the pond and a well had to be sunk to pump more water in

Not perhaps large carp, but beautiful and important fish, well worth saving. The bottom fish has old heron wounds around its shoulders, but hopefully now that the pond has been deepened and refreshed, these attacks will become more and more rare

died; the original puddled clay and chalk bed of the pool was found and preserved intact; and the well filled the entire lake in two weeks. And quite remarkably, though the summer was late, carp began to spawn a second time. This happened nowhere else in the valley, and it was as though these fish realised that their earlier spawning had all been destroyed, that they had to compensate in this way.

The affair of the wild carp at Gallows Hill had unexpected repercussions. Because the Hall had been involved in saving them, the wildies were given a standing previously denied them. Wild carp suddenly became a species of interest and everyone now wanted to talk fish. Quite unexpectedly the valley's MP came to visit, to congratulate and assure us of his sympathies, and the mood in general towards fish and fishermen suddenly altered. Don, with his grasp of public relations, seized on the changed wind and exploited it fully, and for a while we received a whirl of invitations to visit waters and advise their owners. One of these was the old trout lake, a water about which we had long wondered.

We do what we can to rescue fish from the quickly sinking water

Carp with barely water enough to swim in still manage to make their escape. If only they realised what we were trying to do for them

The wild carp spawn again against the dredged banks of their lake

Wandering Whiskers

Late one night in the heat of August, Don knocked and entered the cottage in very agitated mood. He had been fishing beneath the copse bridge around the pool with a worm in the hope of picking up a perch. The river used to be full of them, and there was always the chance of a survivor. The sun had long gone down and it was a very warm, still dusk. Dace were active and the rod tip plucked continually as they pecked at the worms.

Into darkness, and the dace seemed to fade away; the river gurgled at Don's feet, slow, deep and steady. It was then that he had his first serious pull of the evening. He missed it completely, but recast to the same area, four feet down where the pool shallows and speeds a little of the gravel dotted with fallen brickwork. Within only seconds, the rod whiplashed round and Don was on his feet, backwinding and following downstream. Everything went dead. He guessed the fish had connected with the sunken field gate, and though he pulled and pulled, everything went slack.

The upper river still produces the occasional grayling, a beautiful fish that can only live in the purest and most oxygenated of rivers. The grayling is a living barometer of a river's health and every one seen or captured in the upper river gives me a thrill of hope for the future

He tackled up once more and gave it a further hour; but the moon rose, the air turned colder and the river seemed to be quite dead. So now he was here, pondering on the night. The only likely culprit, he decided, could have been a large trout, probably a brown, but just conceivably a sea trout for it was the season when they might be expected. Though nothing like as numerous as immediately post-war, they still run and can be very large. The whole affair interested me greatly: it just rang a tinkle of a far-off bell, so I suggested we return the next morning to examine the stretch in full light.

Happily it was another bright blue day and the river sparkled, so sprightly and clear that we stood just a chance of seeing the bed of the pool. The walk through the wood to the bridge is a long one and the path little used, so it is rare to see an angler on the stone bridge or around the pool. Today, too, the scene was deserted and we began our investigation.

The sunken gate lies twenty yards beneath the tail of the pool and from it, on the top bar, waved three yards of Don's line and, of course, no fish. This made sense, for Don had been cramming on pressure and pulling the fleeing fish to the surface so that it would have hit the old woodwork only six to twelve inches down. Mercifully, the size 8 hook was embedded in the algae-covered wood and not into the flesh of some living fish.

Back by deeper water, we sat ourselves down comfortably and began a long vigil. Seventy per cent of the pool was quite open to our gaze, but the deepest run of water was shadowy and indistinct. Sometimes it gave us a fleeting sight of its bed, when the light breeze was off or the water ran especially smooth, but most of the time it preserved its anonymity. Any fish could be down there, and though we strained we could do no more than make out the vaguest shapes. We were all but sure that they were debris or weed until one gleamed dull gold—and the bell in my head now rang loud and long.

In the late 1970s I had lived in a mill house for a short time on another river, out of the valley altogether. One afternoon a boy had knocked at my door, very excited, with a bucket in his hand: from the millrace he had caught the record gudgeon. The fish in the blue bucket was ten inches long, but it had four barbules not two and it was a tiny barbel, result no doubt of the great spawning year of 1976.

Over the following weeks that year, I caught eighty of these little fish, all on scraps of worm and size 16 hooks, letting the lead bounce through the white water. Some I returned; some I placed up the river; eighteen (or was it twenty?) I brought in two pails to the valley and placed a mile up from the copse where we now stood in excitement. It was not something I should have done but I had felt then the experiment to be worth the risk. It seemed now that perhaps I had been right.

It's strange that once you know what you're looking for you can see it with no difficulty. Where an hour before the pool had looked fishless, now we could see barbel everywhere! They formed a compact shoal of between ten and fourteen fish, and it gratified me to think that so few had been lost, for the dangers facing them had been great. Indeed at the time I had realised that such a scanty stocking was almost doomed to failure, and I was torn between regrets: should I have taken more to the valley? Or should I have left the river totally alone? Now, I had been vindicated.

The underslung mouth and four probing barbules of the barbel all indicate a fish intent in finding food in the bottom gravel, sand and silt. The top lip of the fish particularly gives the game away with its rough nailfile surface, perfectly adapted to grubbing over the small stones to find the larvae and insects beneath

The barbel had remained in the same tight, small group as the day the buckets had been emptied and they had gathered together, gasping in alarm, on the gravels beneath the watercress strands. That day I had watched them for two or three hours until they had sidled in a body away into deeper water and I knew I could do nothing more for them. Never had I expected to see them again, not in the same shoal grown large. It was an immensely satisfying moment.

Especially so when we caught one to examine it. Hooking the fish was easy,

(opposite above) *The nearly beaten barbel still refuses to give up and with its powerful tail fin beats the shallows to a foam.* (opposite centre) *Side strain at last begins to tell and its head breaks water. This is a telling moment for the open mouth takes in air and this makes it more difficult for the fish to return back to deeper water.*

(opposite below) *Beaten at last, the barbel lies beautiful and pristine in the shallow water*

and all these years on, worm did the trick again, bounced along the gravel, through the flashing fish. The take had come in minutes—a full-blooded pull that could not be missed. Landing the fish, however, was another matter. As a seven-incher, the barbeling had struggled: at 7lb it took nearly ten minutes to bring to the shallows.

We were careful not to take it from the water, but simply let it rest on the stones whilst we removed the hook from its bottom lip. All sights in Nature are really above the power of men to describe but I have never felt the inadequacy of my pen more than at this moment. This barbel, uncaught for years, positively glowed.

Neither of us had the slightest desire to catch a second from the shoal, even though a bigger barbel was quite possible: we knew they were there, and that they were flourishing—and that pleased us quite enough. We covered up our tracks and left, careful never to mention the barbel of a copse pool to a single soul.

One of the most spectacularly beautiful barbel I have ever seen and a perfect testament to virgin nature. It is a sad fact that many barbel that are caught are kept in keep-nets and their fins are particularly prone to being caught and ripped in the mesh. Here is a virgin barbel that is absolutely flawless, almost as if it were carved from ivory and varnished mostbeautifully. It was wise not even to land the fish in a net but simply draw it up into shallow water and let it rest, tired, on the smooth pebbles

MARSHLAND LIFE

The Saltings

The estuary, the saltings as the marshes are called, and the sea shore itself, were all of intense interest to us both over our lives. The grey mullet in particular almost destroyed us in the 1970s. Mullet—oh, how that word brings back those years of suffering! Algae grazers that scrape the mud with their rigid top lip for microscopic food; mullet that come and go with the tide, following it in water only inches deep; mullet, lovers of the warmth, fish that overwinter in Spain and follow the summer sun like an eternal tourist; creek mullet that are shadows of the sea and can leap the highest nets, outswim the seals and never, or hardly ever, made an error regarding our baits. For two whole summers we had done little but fish for mullet on every tide that was at all practical—and on many that were not! Often we fished half the night long but, light or dark, our success rate stayed the same: virtually nil. We caught three fish and lost a further couple, despite using every method and bait known to man. We legered, floatfished and span for them. We used bread, maggots, lugworm, ragworm, earthworm, peeler crabs, rice boiled in pilchard oil, shrimps live and dead, chunks of fish and pieces of cheese. Hardly anything seemed to work and the only success we did have was when we pre-baited one particular creek with mashed bread tide after tide. It seemed that the same mullet shoal visited each time and after a week began to recognise the bread as edible. Even so, the fish were very wary of it and bites were too lightning quick to hit more than one in ten.

In short, creek mullet fishing was so frustrating we vowed never to indulge in it again after we had cracked the 5lb barrier with a 6lb 5oz fish. We decided that would do for us, and moved onto far easier fields. Shortly afterwards, I found mullet fishing in harbours, where they are semi-resident and used to feeding on the throwaways of mankind, far more successful. In such places half-a-dozen fish a day are quite possible, but neither the surroundings nor the challenge really compare. If only for its fight, the memory of that six pounder will live with both Don and me for ever. The fish ran almost tirelessly for twenty minutes and jumped repeatedly in the shallow, murky water that lay against the lavender beds. In the end there was discussion as to whether we should eat it, but I remember we both felt such an end totally wrong for such a spirited fish. We let it go and watched it furrow through the shallow water till it disappeared in the deeper water of the creek and swam again with its brothers.

Don had spent first light wandering the channel behind the shingle beach where the river runs to mingle with the sea, 'just to see them run and jump, greyhounds at dawn'. He'd walked there with a spinning rod, throwing out a silver spoon into the surf where the sea trout hunt at night; but fishless, he sat to watch the sunrise and the tide flood the mullet into the marsh. There were thousands of them, and when he cast the spoon into them he could feel it bump the bodies as he retrieved. After three casts he stopped, knowing that they were not following and afraid that he might cause them physical damage. Anyway, he was happy just to sit there, taking in the smell of the salt from the marsh, and feeling the warmth flood into the world.

Two men from the village were passing close by, on their way to the beds of samphire, that strange green marsh asparagus that sells so well to the tourist and tastes so good, hot with butter and black pepper with a round of fresh brown bread. 'Heard you were back,' they called out. 'You have a look at the dykes on your way back. There's fish got in them again after the flood. There's roach and bream that we've seen and what's those fish like roach but all golden? There's a big 'un dead on the far side of Bishop's Marsh, big as a dinner plate 'e is.'

The 1953 flood had brought all manner of horrors. A sad but comparatively small side-effect had been the decimation of the coarse fish populations of the marshes. The sea had overwhelmed them and they had died almost instantly; but Don was hardly surprised at news of their recovery. It was quite likely, too, that they would have a quick growthrate, and he knew that something special might exist; in fact we'd often talked about reconnoitring the marshes but for some reason had always managed to put off the event.

As the sun climbed higher and the tide began to ebb, Don followed the drains back to the coastal road. Frequent shoals of small roach glinted in the sun; brilliantly silver fish with glowing fins, as if the trace of salinity had polished them up like pins. As the samphire pickers had said, there was every chance that these and other species could grow exceptionally large. The brackish water was bursting with shrimp, banks of water-fleas and snails that in their million seemed to relish the pinch of salt.

Don's car was parked by the sluice gates where the river enters the marshes in an intermingled world of sweet and salt water. He turned his back to the sea and looked upriver over the bridge. The last mile was a strange place: during the high tides, weed was killed off by the incoming salt, and there was hardly any flow even at low tide so the water was constantly sluggish, slopping back and forth with little purpose. The river here was wide and shallow and silting up fast. There was little weed cover, and no trees on the banks—these had either been dredged out or been eaten by the cattle. In fact it was a desert tract of water, and what roach did live there had always been traditionally small and wary. Wariness, in fact, was essentially the key to their lives since they were faced with pike, sea trout, otters, herons, terns, gulls and cormorants, to whom roachlings were a delight. The unwary were decimated before their first winter was out, and even for the wary, to live four years was remarkable; hence the fish were always small in that piece of river, and to live the ten years necessary to become big was a most unlikely feat.

All this was in Don's mind as he watched the slowly moving river. It looked absolutely dead to him and the colour of very weak coffee. For a while all he could pick out were slowly moving eels either working their way sinuously through the mid-water zone or shifting themselves into the silt where they could hide the bright daylight hours. Then his attention was caught by a large

Sun up and the tide flooding in, and the mullet run the sea channels

Blanket weed with beds of watercress gather in the big slack on the tidal reach of the river. The water is shallow and slow-moving and tainted with salt. Cover is scarce, but there is still food in plenty for big fish that care to risk the associated dangers

shadow on the bottom, fifty or sixty yards away. It could well have been nothing but weed, but we all know that strange instinct that tells us otherwise. As he approached the shadow moved, apparently able to sense his presence. It was obviously a good fish, but from that distance he could not make out what species it was.

Thus began a chase between fish and man for well over half a mile. The going was easier for the fish—for Don it meant crossing dykes, a swamp and a field of thorns, nettles and brambles, the fish obviously growing more and more uneasy once it realised it was being pursued. Finally Don cut well into an open field and ran a large loop to appear back on the bank, low down in the thistles: the fish lay virtually in front of him. The fish was a roach . . . a super roach . . . a roach Don estimated to be close on 3lb.

From that moment on, it was a fish he wanted dearly, and one he knew would present the most excruciating of challenges. He watched it for a few minutes and then, as its suspicions eased, it turned round and headed back once more for the sluice gates and the sea.

Eel-Netter

It was quite impossible for Don not to want to wet a line before the 16 June; he therefore decided that he must eel fish, and that he would try the Gardener's Pool. 'Try it if you wish, of course,' I said, 'but it was eel-netted about two years ago when a six-pounder was taken away, along with lots of smaller ones between 3 and 4lb.'

'Well, I'll try Gallows Hill then.' 'Netted.' 'The river.' 'That's netted each year.' 'The big lake, then.' 'Netted three years ago, that one.' 'I'll go outside the valley then. I've always fancied Moonstone for a real monster.' 'Don, that's been netted. You've got to realise everywhere's been netted. In many ways it's been a real disaster for the valley.'

As children, Don and I had often biked to Moonstone for the fine rudd there, the small head of big pike and the very large eels. By the end of the day our keepnets would look like treasure troves, with golden red-finned rudd that weighed on average 1lb and a few even topping the 2lb mark. We'd landed pike to nearly 20lb, and of course there was always an eel rod or two leaned against forked sticks, fishing some small deadbait way out in the lake. All eels were decapitated, and were pedalled back home in a bag for the old boys of the village. In those days Moonstone was considered a perfect fishery, and it was hardly surprising that Don's memory of it should be so fresh.

The valley eel-netter had been a keen rod-and-line man once as well, and his knowledge had served him well. His experiences of Moonstone took him and his nets there, and he carted away over two hundred eels from a mere ten-acre water—nearly 600lb weight in all. But the consequences of his drastic action were soon only too obvious, for those old fish that he removed, up to 7¼lb in weight, pythons of things, were more essential than anyone could have guessed. From the next spawning, the decline in Moonstone was unstoppable because now there was nothing to gorge on the eggs of the rudd and the pike, and nothing to feast on the fry and fingerlings as the summer progressed. True, fish fell to the herons and grebes, but from each spawning now thousands more survived and the lake became a mockery of a fishery. Nowhere was a maggot safe from immediate assault by 1 to 3in rudd; and nowhere was such a rudd under a float on a hook safe from a 1 to 3lb pike. Moonstone was now a lake of Lilliput; as a home for fine fish, it had been wiped out.

'That's like a Henry Williamson story I remember,' Don said getting up and crossing to the bookshelves. 'I nearly memorised his books in the city. Him and Jefferies and anyone really who could write well about Nature.' He thumbed around a bit and then began to read:

This rich man, on buying a property, with the keenest of new proprietorship, the new broom, you know, wanted, among other things, a perfect fishery. He began by systematically ridding his river of vermin. He planned it on business lines, step by step. His water bailiffs trapped otters as the biggest enemies. When this had been achieved the river suffered a plague of eels. These he removed by hundreds of baited traps, no doubt by the gross at a considerable trade discount. After a season the bed of his river was over populated by numerous miller's thumbs. These fish are squat, wide mouthed, bald headed and about two inches long. Previous to the mass withdrawal of eels the miller's thumbs had lived under stones, watching for food moving past their hovers.

Now, with no natural enemies except the trout, they multiplied exceedingly. They covered the riverbed eating not only all the trout food, but the eggs of trout as they were laid in October and November, and what fry survived the hatch in February and March.

During the spring and early summer all the squire had in his river was a plague of miller's thumbs and a few enormous bottom feeding trout. These monsters had no progeny and in the course of time all the miller's thumbs were eaten up. The trout were by then too old to spawn, black, gaunt wrecks lay in the water, gradually becoming fungoid and then extinct.

'You see,' Don said, 'this squire had found he was doing just the same thing and ruining the balance of Nature. As time went on Williamson said that he grew more and more depressed until finally he had a vision.' Don shuffled the pages round and began to read again:

. . . now he saw life as an entity: one species absorbing another—water and its fluids into algae into daphne and nymph and so to fry, miller's thumb, eel, heron and otter: and otters occasionally into hounds, whose masters and committee owners are likely to vanish through the new sentiment of the towns where now Jack is as good as his master.

There was yet time to put back the clock and hurrying home he wrote to a firm of zoological collectors, ordering great quantities of miller's thumb's, eels, trout, otters, which in due course were turned into the river. Later he purchased several couples of otter hounds, with which to breed a pack to keep down the otters. These beasts he regularly hunted. Thus the

The eel-netter is a typical man of the country, knowledgeable in all the ways of fish, fowl and animal. Eels are not his only livelihood and a lurcher is quite capable of picking him up a rabbit or two at dawn

status-quo was restored and he, as patron, occasionally squeezed himself in between the balance, and with rod and line passed many a relaxing hour in and beside the water.

'Exactly!' we both said at once, as if telepathically of the same mind.

The story of the eel-netter is strange and sad to relate, particularly in a country community where the eel is regarded with such fascination and awe. In the valley everybody seems to have his own eel story and over the years I've heard them all—eels moving overland, eels choked on ducklings, elvers in the bath-water, eels in water tubs, eels digging up potatoes, eels as long as a man is tall and eels that bark like foxes on heat. And how many times have I heard that eels are best fried, or smoked, or jellied, or cut up and stewed . . . eels, eels, eels: and now they hardly exist *because of this one man*.

Though I am careful to say 'hardly'. 'You remember the old pond that dried up two years back, Don, the tiny one? When that finally became just mud, they found carp struggling in the dregs. They were wildies, around 2 to 5lb, but there were other, larger creatures that the men couldn't catch or even really make out—just shadowy, powerful things stirring up the silt.

The lovely old reels and handmade creels of the Williamson era

'Anyway, two more days of sun and the estate chaps could get right into that last hollow. They picked out a single tench, one large rudd, two more carp and several eels. Five were between 2 and 2½ feet long, and the two largest measured 54 and 55 inches respectively. These two were taken to the bench in the nursery and laid out flat, and the marks are still there where their heads lay—two great big grooves. Now, what on earth would those two eels have weighed? Eight pounds? Nine? Even ten? And who would believe they could exist in a little place like that? And that's what *you've* got to look for now, Don. Somewhere our netsman friend just hasn't considered worth the time or effort, or even somewhere so small he doesn't even know it exists.'

We both thought a while in silence and then I exclaimed: 'The Crucian Puddle!' 'You've got to be joking,' Don said, 'a big eel couldn't fit in there! And it's high up across those chalky hills with no stream to it, so how could eels possibly get in in the first place? No, I think we can forget that one.' 'That's exactly what the netter will have thought,' I took up again. 'OK, there won't be many in there, but I'll bet you anything there's something that will make you sit up.'

Don continued to look unconvinced, so dropping the whole subject of eels I continued: 'If you must fish, why not try for that big trout? He's in season too, like the eels, I suppose strictly you should use a fly but I don't think anyone will really care if you try him with a bait or two.'

No debate this time! Gumboots were soon pulled on and we were away through the wood off to the darkened pool.

The Eelman's Work

'That roach was probably twenty or twenty-five years old, even more,' I said of his big upper river fish. 'From what you've described, the lesions and scale damage were almost certainly the result of columnaris and the outbreak we know about took place about twenty years back . . . although, I suppose it's possible there have been more isolated eruptions of it since. You said it looked an old fish though . . . perhaps if you'd taken a scale reading you'd have helped prove something . . .'

Talking about coarse fish in any biological depth has always been a problem. Roach, for example, have never represented money in the way of salmon or trout and have therefore been largely neglected by researchers who in their turn need funding. Who, or what organisation, would finance research into roach or perch, or any other non-economically productive species, for long enough for a study to be conclusive? The professionals of fishery science have themselves always been required to research their master's choice rather than follow their own wishes. What we know about roach, is, as a result, largely the result of passionate amateurs. We know what, when and how they eat, and how fast they grow, but it is the important details that we lack—for example, one might assume that the perch disease and columnaris are perhaps Nature's regulatory forces, checking over-proliferation, but we don't know that for sure.

The roach is very probably Britain's most popular coarse fish and yet a great deal of its intimate biology remains a secret. Walton called it 'river sheep' which could have been accurate in long ago days of plenty. Now, however, a large river roach is one of the most sought-after of angling triumphs

However does this actually matter? 'Read this, Don.' And I showed him an important piece written by Drew Young, one of the few trained biologists passionate about the coarse species:

The perch disease is a very emotional subject amongst those of us that love coarse fishing; just try to take a step back, look at the problem rationally, and ask yourself this question: if we manage to identify a single organism that caused perch disease, what would we do with that knowledge?

   Would we vaccinate perch? Treat fisheries with antibiotics? Ban angling on waters which might be affected? Shoot seagulls, terns, ducks, swans and geese? None of these is practical. Not even remotely possible. Ask yourself how many viral or bacterial pathogens have been eradicated. The prospect of defeating this perch disease organism is nil. What can we do then? We can support the A.C.A. We can join the environmental groups and work within them to keep our waters and all waters clean. We could join any political

A quite perfectly shaped and coloured roach. This is probably a new fast-growing fish around eight or nine years of age, with perhaps another three or four years of growth in front of it. It is a fish like this that is going to make one of the big three-pounders of the future

party that would put environmental matters before the pursuit of profit and help them develop their policies so that anglers are seen as guardians of the countryside and not as animal abusers.

When the perch disease strikes, we know from history that the perch will return. Radioactivity and toxic pollution may destroy fisheries for ever. I am sure that if we can only look after the water environment, our good friends the perch will look after themselves.

The Book of the Perch, the Perch Fishers 1990.

'Environmental matters before the pursuit of profit,' Don repeated. 'If only. What chance of that? We can only expect platitudes of governments or corporations, yet all our fish are sensitive to everything the river brings them— they can't escape it, and if the sewage farm breaks down or the carrot factory goes wrong they are dead and gone for ever. Yes, he's quite right that the essential thing is to control the environment, and not to worry unduly about a disease.'

It was sharply brought home to us just how vulnerable our coarse fish are, on Don's second trip to the upper river some eight days later. He had been unable to relocate the roach shoal until then, but on another warm, bright day he struck lucky about half a mile from the bridge. The first thing he noticed was that only about half the shoal was present—fifteen or perhaps twenty fish at most. More pleasing was that a few of the smaller fish, those of around 2lb, seemed quite happy to feed and take the drifting pieces of flake, slowly at first, then after half an hour virtually everything was gobbled. It was quite a simple matter to put up the 13ft rod with no floats or weights, and cast just a piece of flake on a size 12 hook. A 2lb 2oz roach intercepted it immediately and was hustled out with a minimum of splash or annoyance to the other shoal members. In fact they remained quite calm, and Don was confident of a second fish the same day.

However, before he could make another stalk a boat with an outboard motor chugged past and the shoal scattered completely. The man on the engine showed no interest in Don who saw that the boat was stacked with black dustbins. He was apprehensive and followed the boat at a distance. A mile upstream it stopped in a lonely piece of aldercarr, and rather as Don had feared, the boatman began to pull in eel-nets. Don quickened his pace through the nettles and as he closed in he saw to his horror, dace, pike and big roach being dropped back over the side into the river. The current washed the badly injured dace past him, and this was quite enough to make Don explode. His resentment over the eel decline had been building up, and now to find the other half of the roach shoal incarcerated and probably wounded made his blood quite boil over.

Evidently it was a pretty ugly scene; in no uncertain terms Don told the man what he'd do to the nets if he ever found them again . . . and probably what he'd try to do to the netsman himself. Certainly the eelman's truck was not seen on the river bridge again that year, but the episode was a sour one and Don's day had turned from triumph to disaster. The sadness was made even worse when four days later, he found the shoal reunited but with at least a third of the fish carrying noticeably fresh-looking scars—the monster itself had a sore and still bleeding nose. In despair, Don abandoned the shoal for the rest of the summer in the hope that they would repair themselves in peace and tranquillity. He had not, however, forgotten the big roach of the tidal reaches, a challenge temporarily shelved but certainly not declined.

Eel Affairs

As the summer developed my interest in eels grew quickly, especially as the very clear water conditions and the long hours of sunshine allowed close scrutiny. If it is at all possible, I grew very close to one eel at the Gardener's Lake whilst I plotted the fall of the Buddha. The Gardener's Lake had no small fish for the eel to prey on and yet it had grown large, a fabulous dark brown creature perhaps a yard long. For an hour at a time it would drift, swirl and gorge in the daphnia, just like the great leather carp fifteen yards from it. The snout of the eel was narrow and its mouth worked constantly as it sucked in the minute organisms or plucked at the blanket weed, tugging it, shaking it to release the tiny items clinging there and to throw them back into the open water where they could be eaten. For all its life long in the Gardener's Lake the eel had presumably absorbed only such tiny foods as these, and not the dead fish, frogs or ducklings of common imagination. Indeed, the one time I attempted to catch it I tried two lobworms on a size 4, and these proved quite a failure. Even after five or ten minutes of puffing and blowing and chewing and champing the eel had only managed to get a quarter of the bait in its mouth.

I got to quite love that eel, so far from the sinister image of a fish lying amongst branches and brickwork waiting for the night and its meal of fish and flesh. This was a true fish, an active, swimming, free-feeding fish, as catchable on maggots as a roach or a perch. It always inhabited the same hole, sometimes invisible for a while as it rested in thick blanket weed, but soon, however, to emerge, gorging as before, head swaying in the ever present daphnia cloud. I could only guess why the daphnia were always present in that place: light values, weed growth, water temperature and currents were presumably attractive; and whilst there was food, there was no need for the eel to move, and so it remained.

The summer continued to bake, and as July gave into August I began to notice more eels in the Gardener's Lake. Whereas before, my eel and perhaps a dozen others would be all that I would see week in and week out, the sight now of a score of eels was common. On one particular day I counted at least thirty different fish around the margin where there were gaps in the weed. It was also interesting that virtually all of these new eels had much broader heads than my own particular pet fish, which remained where it was and quite aloof from the intruders in its lake. I managed to feed these fatter-headed fish on worms easily, on small roach from the other lakes and even, once, on a piece of freshly shot rabbit. Food that my eel would have ignored was greedily consumed. What was also noticeable was that the big-headed eels ate more irregularly. A small roach for example would generally be ignored, but if it *was* eaten, the eel would come back for two or three more similar-sized fish. Equally, when a big lobworm was taken the fat-headed eel would go on scavenging until it had made a real meal of them. In short, the two eel types appeared to have totally differing lifestyles, and presumably because of this they could cohabit happily together in a single water without competing for the other's food. What, in fact, these broad-headed eels found to eat in the Gardener's Lake puzzled me. There were a few crawfish to be sure, and the odd frog or newt and the like, but as already mentioned, the water was pretty well devoid of small fish. If it was a mystery where these new eels had come from, it was also difficult to understand how they would flourish.

I mentioned these facts to the gardener himself, I asked around at The Swallows and up and down the valley generally, but it seemed that the only person able to answer my question would be the eel-netter himself; though disliking the prospect thoroughly, I decided to go and see him. His cottage lay in a back lane two miles from the sea and the sheds around it were draped in nets, traps, boxes, long lines, and every sort of eel-catching necessity. The man himself was at breakfast when I arrived, a very late one as he told me, for the nets had to be pulled in around sunrise and all the traps sorted before he could call a piece of the day his own. He did not seem at all surprised at my question.

'It's the hot summer, my beauty,' he replied. 'Let me tell you I'm catching double the weight now I was back in May or June. What's happening in your old pond is going on everywhere. You see, as the summer dries up the fields, the drainage dykes and the ditches they all be losing their water, too. What most people don't know is that a lot of eels live in these places for most of the year, but now they're having to move out to the nearest standing water. Everyone thinks of eels as a fish plain and simple but there's more to it than that. They need some water, for sure, but some of them travel miles, not over actual dry land mind, but along any ditch where there's damp. You'll find them living there off the fat of the land—worms by the ton, toads, newts, frogs and spawn, loaches and sticklebacks. They get big in there without any need of anything else. There's always food for them. What's happening now is that the *ditches* are drying, and the eels are getting the hell out fast while they've got the chance, and not all of them end up in the water that suits them a great deal. Once the rains come at the back end though they'll be off again, at least until the winter comes in very cold.'

'What then?'

'Don't know, boy. I'm frying other fish then!' He laughed a good deal then at the discomfiture on my face. 'Don't you worry. The valley's big enough for the two of us, lad. Mind your business and I'll keep to mine. In that way we'll get on well together.'

A protesting eel comes to the net, its head buried in weed

The stile leads to the eel-netter's cottage

Don's Dyke

Carnival day in August 1969 was good to us. I had come third in the greasy pole competition and, more importantly, I had survived. Don's success was to come second in the race out to the coastguard's house and back, a round trip of about ten miles in all. Engines were not permitted, so competitors canoed, sailed or sometimes set out on horseback. Don conceived the fiendish combination of cycling, running, rafting and swimming. The raft was to carry him over the deep, dark freshwater dyke behind the sea-wall and was a master stroke, for no one ever fancied swimming it. It was deep and black-looking, surrounded by reeds and all but covered in green flannel weed. Thereafter, locals knew the place as young Don's dyke.

Around that time we had fished the dyke but only half-heartedly, for to reach it involved a major trek over foul-smelling muds; and though there were rumours of bream and perch even, all we ever got there were eels, flounders and a solitary sea trout . . . and how that got in there we never could work out.

However, our recent conversation with the samphire pickers had not been forgotten. Before 1953 there had been reports of rudd—good rudd—in the dyke, and somehow rudd and the tang of salt had always gone together. Slapton Ley, Hickling Broad, Heigham Sound . . . so why not our own marsh, we reasoned? I was completely lost to the Buddha at that time, but Don was keen on revisiting the scene of his childhood triumph—though I did advise him to clear things with the warden before setting out. The marshes are an ornithologist's Mecca and closely controlled, and a human figure can be seen for miles against the lonely, table-flat marshland. As I expected, the warden was helpful. He had seen rudd himself, pretty good ones, and all he asked was that Don went in the evening during the week when bird-watchers would be scarce. So at 7pm Don set out along the course of his race so many years ago: then it had taken him eleven minutes to reach the dyke; now he anticipated a forty-minute walk. For that reason he travelled light with just a rod, a bag of tackle and bait, and a camera slung around his neck.

It was a golden evening. On his left as he walked along the marsh path, the tide was in and a flotilla of dinghies tacked here and there in the beam of the slowly sinking sun. There were odd splashes as mullet leaped, chased by grey seals, and the lavender smelled strongly and clearly. The dyke itself seemed much smaller to him, partly due to time magnification and partly because the reed fringe had grown out much further. Now probably only half the water was open, but that at least still looked fresh and clear. In fact there was only one possible swim to fish from, and from there any hooked fish would have to be guided very carefully in past the towering reeds. Don mashed up some bread and threw it two rod lengths out, just beyond the vegetation line. He plumbed the spot, found it was seven feet and set the float six inches over depth. Out went the hooked flake, and he waited.

Nothing happened. For over an hour the dyke looked very dead indeed and he grew tempted to put on a worm and try for a couple of flounders for tea. The first worm produced an eel of six inches and the second worm one of 1lb. Not even a flounder could he get, and his attention again wandered into the past . . . an owl floated over the marshes and ghosted the bank of the dyke, and Don watched it through his binoculars. Then, just on the fringe of his lens sights, the end of a ripple came into view. Sitting down he had seen no disturbance, for the reeds obscured his view, so now he stood up to see better.

Gaining a little height up an old post he could see the disturbances clearly, and the binoculars told him their reason. Crusts in the mashed bread had obviously broken off, floated to the surface and been pushed down the pool by the delicate evening breeze. Half-way down the dyke, fish had found them and were feeding upon them—the sun showed up their glints of gold and red clearly—and then in full view of the field glasses, a monstrous rudd heaved

The world of the Saltings is a beautiful one; a third sea, a third land and a third sky. It is vulnerable to tides and to floods but there is a great fertility in the soil and in the areas of brackish or sweet water that allow coarse fish to grow quickly to a great size. This is not unusual, and along many of the coasts of Britain dykes and lagoons produce very big tench and rudd, in a type of environment frequently overlooked by the specialist angler

himself clear and held a second, poised on pectorals, before wallowing away.

A small carp controller float, a size 8 hook and a thumbnail piece of crust reached the required distance, and within three minutes his rod was bent hard to keep a heavy fish from the reeds.

'That's a piddly one, boy.' In the drama the warden had come up behind him unobserved. Don had just recorded a weight of 3lb and simply gawped . . . at the beauty of the fish, at the unexpected visitor, at the impact of his comment. 'There's fish twice his size, don't you worry.'

Well, there weren't. Not that we saw, even though we tried hard. We did find Don's old raft in the reed, patched it up a little and explored the dyke thoroughly until it broke up under our weight, getting us wet one fortunately very hot day. A 6lb rudd . . . I still dream. Imagine it! Such a fish would dwarf the sun.

The magnificent rudd is held against the evening light

VALLEY PREDATORS

———— Thoughts On Valley Perch ————

Talk frequently turned to the perch—no coarse fisher can deny what a good sort of fellow the perch is— and Don had not felt the tug of a big one since the early 1970s. Over the decades I have seen good perch come from every water in the valley—probably, in my time, I have caught or witnessed the capture of almost 250 perch of between 2 and 3lb, and seen a good many more in the water. One particular perch shoal which frequented the river island in 1966 numbered then around 500 strong, where not a fish was less than a pound and most were double that. In fact, 2 to 2½lb has always seemed to have been the normal ceiling for those fish which have progressed beyond the fingerling stage, but there have been monsters. The 6lb giant at Wood Pigeons Lake was not so far ahead of the big fish that lived through the late 1950s by the sluice gates where the river meets the estuary. I saw that fish several times one summer and it was vast and golden, constantly surrounded by schools of tiny roach, perch, elvers and shrimps. In fact, there was so much food around it that it became impossible to catch, and stories went that eventually it was found, washed up dead on the mud-flats. There was also the huge fish that lived in the late 1960s under the road bridge; when finally caught, it was said to weigh 4lb 7oz. And there was another valley perch I lost one Christmas Eve which was undoubtedly 4lb plus. Extraordinary fish all of them, from the past when so many aspects of life seem bigger and better—but there are perch now and there will be in the future. As I see it, and I told Don this, so much in recent years has been made of the perch disease, but in the valley perch populations tell a less dramatic and more cyclical story. Oh yes, the perch disease does exist. The red sores and the fish dying in their hundreds have been seen here as everywhere, but taken in an historical sweep of eighty years—the longest anyone can recall in the valley—the disease has only been a part of a long-standing pattern. This is what I learned from a dozen fishermen, old boys perhaps but with razor-sharp memories, and some old photographs or even a few scribbled records with dates and weights.

Of course this was never a consciously documented history but it *was* possible to make some sense of it all: what I deduced to my own satisfaction, after long study, is that perch waters are unusually volatile, that big perch are fast-growing and short-lived, and that a strong year-group of big perch can be here one season and utterly devastated and dead the next. It seems that all the waters in the valley lie fallow for years with a small population of little perch simply on tick-over. The species remains ever present but never makes an impact of any sort . . . until quite out of the blue, big perch appear again. It is as though the water has been fallow all these years just waiting to explode. Perhaps an unusually strong year-class emerges. Perhaps a good breeding year for the roach and bream provides a plenitude of spawn for the small perch, and

A stunning perch, all bristling hostility, the supreme hunter of the small fish

The typical perch, even a small one like this, is all aggression. The dorsal fin is erect and the pectorals are on the go. The big eyes have seen a shoal of small fish moving above and the perch is beginning to assume its attack position

then fry and fingerlings for the fast-growing predators. Once these perch have had this headstart and become weaned to their fish diet, then their growth is rapid and guaranteed.

This seems to have been the case decade after decade up and down the valley both in river and in stillwater. For the greater part of the century there have been occasional, isolated eruptions of big fish and sometimes this has happened through all the waters at once, suggesting a common factor such as ideal weather and fertile spawning years.

The greed of small piscivorous perch is an amazing sight. A 4-inch perch can eat thirty to forty fry over a twenty-four hour period, a whole miniature shoal in fact. A group of fast-growing, fish-eating perch will eat tens of thousands of fry during the course of the summer and autumn, and the spawning must be particularly prolific to be able to sustain them. Like eels, perch have in the valley's past been central in pruning roach and rudd stocks, and big roach and rudd have almost invariably been linked with either healthy eel or perch populations or both.

Indeed, it seems possible that the thinning out of eels by eel-netting might just help a perch comeback. Perhaps a lessening of competition around the spawning beds might help the small perch get a toe-hold and move up the ladder to a good size.

A very lovely perch goes back to the water. Though it has been caught and unhooked, there is no visible sign that an angler has ever touched it. The fins and scales are perfect and hopefully the fish will have undergone minimum stress

But how the perch had prospered thereafter, I did not know for sure. There were tantalising rumours, but so there always are around perch stocks, and the last live perch of over 1lb that I'd actually seen had been a couple of years back, so I had no positive advice to offer. I simply suggested to Don that he should keep an open mind, and realise that perch could appear anywhere at any time; and to watch out for the simplest things.

Waters where small perch proliferate are always worth deeper investigation. Any sign of a striking predator should be studied closely as well. Perch hunt in packs rather than singly so if a shoal of prey lifts up, harassed from several quarters, then pike are unlikely aggressors. The commotion an attacking perch makes is less than that of a pike, simply due to the difference in size, but is often more splashy. Also, perch are more prone to hunting the single fish than pike who prefer the short sharp dash. A perch, by contrast, will chase ten yards or more, slowing the fish down by tiring it and injuring it with snaps to the tail. A perch probably does not choose to hunt like this. Rather, like a trout, he has not the shovel head and formidable mouth of the pike, and has to compromise a little in his hunting method.

None of this was a great help to a man desperate to clap eyes on a big perch again after a gap of nearly twenty years, and in fact, Don's single perch of the year was to fall in a less than typical way.

A perfect perch, just touching two pounds in weight. The dorsal fin is seen clearly; a banner, rather like the skull-and-crossbones flag, proclaiming it the pirate of the pool

This is a rather lean fish caught, interestingly, from a water where many of the small fish were netted out and taken to other pools outside the valley. The owner felt his water was overstocked but the removal of small fish obviously began to have an immediate effect on the predator populations. Water management is obviously a good thing but every single factor has to be taken into account before Nature's balance is interfered with

An Unusual Result

The trout lake lies deep in the wood and has been utterly neglected for over five years. Branches have fallen into it and the path to it has become overgrown and wild. Both Don and I remembered it as the place where as boys we learned to poach. Trout were stocked there regularly in those days: at least twice a year the tractor and trailer would push through the wood with the two great galvanised tanks that held a hundred or so brown trout each. We'd see the tractor and the owner in his Land-Rover depart, but would still lie low; only when they had faded totally out of earshot would we get to work with our poker rods, our sturdy lines and our hooks alive with garden worms.

All this was a long time ago, but the stockings had continued until the farmer's death, just six years before. Since then the lake had fallen into a beautiful and wild neglect, and several things had happened to the water. The browns had lingered on for a while, some grown large and lank with thinning bodies and big, almost dog-tooth heads, though it would be doubtful if any still existed now. The second event of note was that a flash flood four summers back had swept some rudd down the valley. By all accounts these had settled in well to the old trout lake, had spawned and were thriving. Finally, it had been some years since the pike had been culled and now there was a proliferation of jacks. Those few that still fished the old lake had told me that a 5lb pike was now considered a good fish there— and for that reason I have kept well clear of the place!

However, there was—as there always had been—one niggling doubt, because for years there had been a legend of a great she-wolf pike in the water. The disappearance of any number of duck and ducklings was laid to her account and the keeper, the farmhands and the farmer himself all swore to seeing the large swirls of water and the few telltale floating feathers.

Now that Don and I were actually invited to fish the lake, the old pike again reared her head. If such a great fish existed, would she still now be alive? Without the constant feeding of free trout, wouldn't such a large fish have gone back dramatically in condition? Or would it be possible for a great female to feed on the new influx of rudd and indeed on the numerous small jacks, probably her very own children? We were agreed that if the pike *were* there, then she would probably be easy to catch since her experience of anglers and tackle must surely have been limited; very probably a carefully fished trout would remind her of past feasts and pleasures.

Our plan was a simple one: on a wet October day we transported a dozen tiny rainbow trout to the water. The largest bait was some six inches, and we felt sure that a day swimming these around the lake untethered under a small float would provoke the big fish, should there be one.

We took no chances with the tackle, for should the great fish exist and be hooked we did not want to risk losing her in the tree branches that ringed the water. Rods were 12ft with a powerful 3lb test curve, and the spools of the reels were loaded with 15lb line. The trebles were solid, forged size fours with the barbs tucked in a little. The pike that could destroy gear like this would be a fish indeed! We greased our lines liberally so that they floated well and offered little resistance to the working live baits. Just small bombs near the hooks kept these baits down a little and stopped them splashing day long on the surface, though the occasional disturbance from them would do no harm whatsoever.

(opposite above) *A brown trout bears the marks of pike teeth. The link between trout and pike is notorious and certainly on stocked trout waters pike, if not culled, can grow to enormous sizes. It is possible that the trout provide a high protein surplus to the normal pike's diet but it is also a fact that a stewpond fish is less adept to the ways of the wild and is therefore more easily caught by the predator. The one-pound stocked rainbow trout therefore represents an easy nutritious meal and, if there are enough of them, fast pike growth is guaranteed*

(opposite below) *The summer often ends in an orgy of straw burning. This practice happily at last is beginning to die out. A great amount of insects perish and where the feeds adjoin rivers or pools there is no doubt that fish food stocks do suffer*

From the start the day looked like being a disaster. Within two minutes my float went and a 2lb jack was found to be the culprit: a few minutes on, and Don claimed a four-pounder; by ten o'clock we had one trout still alive in our bucket and the biggest pike was still the four-pounder. By noon we were quite desperate. We had to resort to catching small rudd to bait our hooks and they, if anything, had reduced the size of our captures. It was now rare to catch a pike above 2lb and by three o'clock in the wet afternoon I was all for an early return home. Don, though, would not hear of it. With the evening approaching fast, he reasoned that if a big fish were there, and were to strike, our time was surely coming.

Four o'clock. Six tiny pike later and Don had the fortune to catch one that threw up a still-quite-fresh rainbow trout! He regarded this as something of a gift from the gods and immediately put it on his tackle, pushed the float up the line and legered the bait well out in the middle of the lake.

Whilst I continued to catch and sacrifice the continuing stream of small rudd, Don's float sat out there unmolested. That in itself was quite a fine thing, for it was the first time all day that either of us had failed to have a run within ten minutes! Thankfully, the light now was failing fast; I had begun to pack my second rod away and was beginning to move with happy purpose towards the one still fishing. Before I reached it, however, Don called out that his dead bait was at last on the move.

There is a sixth sense in anglers that tells them when something special is about to happen, and I was quite convinced as Don tightened to the

A small pike comes to hand, captured this time on a plug

disappearing float and struck that he would be in to the great pike—I fully expected his rod to take on a forbidding curve as it met the sullen power of a really heavy old fish. I was therefore massively disappointed when nothing out of the ordinary happened, and the rod simply nodded as what appeared to be yet another jack began the procession into the bank. A little way out it gave something of a spirited run, enough to make us think the four-pound barrier might just have been broken.

By this time we weren't bothering with nets, and I turned my back to let Don scoop the jack out by hand. Then a cry: 'Good God!' I turned round to see one of the biggest perch I have ever seen flapping on the fallen leaves. The dead trout was flung clear of its jaws and it lay free and perilously close to the waterline. Don was on it in a flash, cradling it with hoops of joy: nearly 4lb, his big perch at last.

We tramped home through the wood still laughing and talking, eager as the boys of years ago. Out of courtesy, we stopped at the keeper's cottage to thank him for our day and tell him about our success. He was warm in his welcome and brewed us both a very satisfying cup of tea. He did not seem at all impressed by the perch; all he was interested in was that pike, the great pike, a pike he claimed to have seen only a month before: a huge pike like a telegraph pole, like a sunken boat, that he'd seen off and on for half a century.

The Survivor

Throughout the summer Don had kept seeing a very good pike in the river. On most of his journeys there it had passed him, always on the move, and generally so quickly it was impossible to follow or to put a bait to, even if he had had the necessary tackle with him. Just occasionally the fish drifted past slowly on the speed of the current, but its usual pace was that of a man walking and the small fish would shear out in front of it, marking its course until out of sight. Though a nice fish, it was not huge by inflated modern standards; simply its whole aura made it attractive to Don. It was a chunky, apparently deep fish, easily recognised by its extreme lightness of colour and vivid yellow spotting, and it had a look about it of infinite power and grace. Certainly the surge that carried it up or down the river was awesome.

There were at least a couple of points of interest about this fish. Firstly, its very size was a question worthy of debate. The river had never previously produced many good fish, for there were just too many problems for them to face. Jacks proliferated up to 6lb but fish very much above that weight had very rarely been seen for decades. The eel-netter obviously tended to take pike away when he found them, and then there were also the village boys who delighted in catching the small pike on the crudest of tackle—almost invariably they would flatten their skulls with a rod rest or branches. My preachings to them had had only some effect, for country traditions were strongly bred and the chance of a few bob extra, because the pike were extremely saleable in the village, was hard to resist. Natural predation by eels on the fry and waterfowl on the fingerlings was also intense, but it was probably human pressures that over the years had accounted for the relatively small size of the river pike. How and why this particular fish remained at large was something of a mystery.

The extreme mobility of the pike was no more easy to understand. Indeed, Don calculated that on many days the fish travelled at least four miles and possibly more, and showed very little inclination to lie in ambush for the dace shoals in the way of the smaller pike. We wondered if it had latched on to a particular shoal of dace and was only interested in following them in their wanderings up and down the river. This, however, made no sense at all, for the dace shoals, by comparison, seemed fairly stable in their position and only really moved any distance on a seasonal basis. Possibly its size and its nomadic nature were linked. Perhaps human persecution, from an early age of awareness, had kept it on the move. Certainly its reluctance to lie any length of time in the recognised pike lairs must have accounted for its longevity to some extent. Obviously, there were recognised hotspots on the river where a pike could hardly lie at rest and stood an almost daily chance of being taken by one of the more youthful members of the unofficial village fishing society. In the pool by the bridge, for example, it is doubtful whether any pike could have survived more than a few months without being caught, speared or snared in some way and, by using the more remote areas of the river, the big pike must have increased his chances of survival. Don also noticed that there seemed to be some correlation between the pike's movements and the early summer appearance of the eel-netter. Certainly he never saw the pike near either the man, the boat or the nets, and we decided that the pike had possibly had a brush with the eelman in the past and had retained some memory of it.

This particular fish was not to be easily caught by Don himself, either. When Don set about the task in October he felt that it would not take him long to accomplish, but he turned out to be very wrong indeed. In part at least, Don's continuing failures could be put down to the water conditions. The October leaf fall had soured the water to an extent and despite quite heavy rain the river still ran summer-clear. So depleted was the chalk strata beneath the river that it would take many months of rain before the ground was full and saturated and a normal flood could take place. As it was, rain simply assisted the wind in chilling the water and slowing the entire cycle of life. The river, furthermore, *seemed* exceptionally prolific in dace that particular autumn; though this was probably because the weed was dying back so they were all the more visible. And, of course, if Don could see them so much more clearly then presumably it would be much easier for a hungry pike to hunt them.

On one particular afternoon, Don found his pike hanging motionless in a slack. This appeared to be a golden opportunity which Don was quick to seize. Settling many yards away upriver, he worked a 4in dace down to where the pike lay. There Don stopped the bait and let it work round in front of the pike's nose for some five minutes. The pike showed little interest and eventually melted away downriver. Very carefully Don inspected the area and found the pike again at the foot of the eddy some three feet beneath the surface. The dace was manoeuvred around to this second position, but no sooner had the frantic, silver fish appeared within the pike's vision than it bolted with a great bow-

The summer river meanders through the old woods and past an old boat

wave upriver. That the pike would so clearly have nothing to do with this particular ruse suggested that very probably it had been hooked and returned or, more probably, lost once or twice as a jack, and still remembered very clearly what tackle looked like and what effect it had on the action of a prey fish.

Would a dead bait work better? We felt not in the clear cold water. Would fishing at night perhaps allay the pike's suspicions and lull it into a false sense of security? We reasoned that possibly it had never been fished for after dark—though the chances of Don contacting it were so slim as to be discounted. Perhaps the pike was not eating dace at all, but had in actual fact turned to another favoured diet. We discussed the possibility of using eel for bait, or roach; but this latter, in particular, Don could not bring himself to do. What did remain possible was the scaling down of tackle, and using gear as light as possible considering the river and the size of the fish being pursued.

Consequently, Don decided on a small bait, small trebles, a small float, 8lb line and the lightest trace that he could get away with. With this revised approach, he set about trotting the river and covering as much water as possible, rather than stalking the fish and hunting it individually. Several dozen jack pike later this plan was also abandoned.

It then began to occur to Don that conceivably this particular pike was feeding *actually on the move*, and that the fish that scattered in front of it were not merely being alarmed, but were being chased. Accordingly, on a bright day at the end of October, he set himself to look for the fish, and after nearly eight hours on the river was successful. It was working slowly upstream about two feet beneath the surface, and Don dropped a small dace some couple of yards above its head. The pike looked immediately interested, quickened its pace and made a quite definite stab at the dace, missing in its haste. However, as

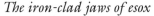

The iron-clad jaws of esox

A superbly marked pike is returned to the water absolutely unharmed

Don expected it to do, the pike did not go back for the unfortunate fish but continued its way upstream. Don wound in and continued the pursuit. A hundred yards upriver a second opportunity presented itself, though this time Don removed the float so that the dace was actually free-swimming. This made all the difference. Finding the pike closing in on it, the dace actually swam quite quickly away from it upriver and the pike was fired into another attack. This second time there was no mistake, the pike was firmly hooked, and the light gear proved quite adequate in handling a good fish that fought surprisingly well.

On the bank the pike was every bit as attractive as it had ever looked in the water, and Don was highly relieved to find that the single barbless treble was only just lodged inside the top jaw and came away without any trace of blood or disfigurement. The pike was very heavily built and Don was surprised that his estimate of 16 to 17lb was out by over 10 per cent. At 19lb 3oz the fish was one of the biggest from the river, certainly since the 1940s. As he slipped it back, Don prayed that the unusual lifestyle that the pike had evolved might keep it safe until it had grown well into the twenties, or at least had lived out its natural span.

Poikey Pie

About five years before, Tom, the landlord of The Swallows, had died quite suddenly; his wife had carried on gamefully for a couple of years but the strain was too great and the pub was sold. It was 'renovated' into a 'modern/old' hostelry, though visitors who had not known the old benches, the little hatched bar and the flat, strong keg bitter of old might well have thought they had stumbled onto the genuine article. Beer, however, became more expensive overnight: Tom, after all, had worked on the fields and did not see the pub as his sole bread and butter. Nor were the old boys who nursed a half pint encouraged quite as they had been before. Such lowly consumption was not guaranteed to pay off the mortgage, and nor was the 'pub grub' of Tom's day: sandwiches the size of a doorstep for a couple of pence. Food now was fancy, the sort of 'country fare' that no countryman could afford: pheasant, beef and venison, all casseroled with exotic sauces, the recipes in languages no valley woman would ever ever be able to understand.

Truth to tell, Don and I hardly ever glanced at the blackboard menu behind the beer taps. We were drinkers pure and simple and only by chance, at the turn of November, did we notice anything untoward.

'What does that say?' Don asked me. 'Poikey Pie'! 'Poikey? Landlord, what does 'poikey' mean?' 'Pike, chaps. We make a very nice pie out of it. No bones. Nicer than trout, I think. You're fishermen, you'd like it.' 'Pike.' '*Pike!*' 'Who supplies it?' 'Well, you know the eelman. A pound a pound. Dirt cheap compared with any other fish. That's how I can do the thing for the price I can.' 'Him!' 'Yes. Seems he's sending a lot to London and places and I'm quite lucky to get any at all. There's a big demand for it. All this green scare, I suppose. Since all the chemicals and antibiotics have been exposed in sea fish and farm-bred trout, natural fish are quite in demand. The North Sea's just a pit of mercury and God knows what. I should think he's cleaning up with these and the eels too.'

Both of us visited the eelman's cottage this time.

He was not at home, and we waited through the short autumnal afternoon. The falling leaves were affecting Don greatly: the summer had visibly departed, and I think it depressed him to learn that the valley was not the idyll he had dreamt it to be. I hoped his depression was a passing phase, for his presence had been of enormous help to me: to find a man as committed as I to the understanding of the valley had been a comfort and stimulus.

Finally, the easily recognised truck pulled into the drive. In the gloom we saw the eelman unloading several sacks and nets and as we walked across the bodies of several pike spilled out onto the gravel. 'What the hell . . .' I held Don back and the eelman grunted. 'Here again are you, with your tender consciences?'

'Conscience is nothing to do with it. You simply have no right to do all this. It's a complete and utter rape of waters that are dear to a lot of people. They don't belong to you and you're taking fish that don't belong to you. You're a bloody thief!'

A fight is not the right word for what followed. Rather it was a scuffle, but we soon ran out of steam and stood angrily glaring at each other. 'Best come in,' the eelman said, rubbing his knuckles.

'You sit and go on about natural balance and the role of the predator, but you just see it from your own point of view. All right, so there haven't ever been big pike in the valley. Not for years, 'cos if I weren't netting them then Dad was, or Granddad was, or his dad was. There's allus been eelmen in this cottage, and if we weren't netting eels in the spring it would be crabs at sea or pike in the winter. That's how we live, boys, and that's that. What *you* do is a bit of pleasure. What we've allus done is fish to *live*, us and our families.

There'll be fish here long after I'm gone. I'm hardly going to take them all today and starve tomorrow, am I? They might not be the big owd sods you two is after, but that's just what you want yourselves. Plenty of boys are glad enough to catch the little eels I stock up with, and taking out the pike now and again only means more small ones for them. Who's right? I don't know, but I'm not stopping now. Not on your lives I'm not.'

I was quiet through all this, but when finally the eelman finished talking I asked him what was the most saleable size of pike that he took away. 'About 5 to 6lb.'

A compromise presented itself to me. 'If we can't stop you taking pike, then will you at least return any over 7 or 8lb? That way Nature could get the larger predators that she needs, and you'd still make your living. If you look at it this way, you are an enormous predator and you must be upsetting the balance to some extent. At the moment you are the head of the food chain on many of these waters and just putting back some of the better pike would help enormously.'

'And you'd get the big fish that you want.'

'Yes, but that's not our biggest object in all this.'

'I'm not saying yes or no, but I'll think on it. I will. And seeing as you've come like, you know I don't fish the new pit don't you?' We didn't. 'It's a wildfowl sanctuary or some such nonsense and I'd be shot if I was seen on there. Mind you, it's old enough to have big pike in it. And eels and all sorts. Get permission there and you'd be well off, I'd say.'

Out of this nettle danger . . .

We left only half satisfied. Don especially was very reluctant to believe a compromise possible, and the whole affair continued to trouble him.

The eel-netter and dog spy us from afar

VALLEY POOLS

— *Strange Happenings At The Crucian Puddle* —

For us, the fishing season proper actually began in a most peculiar way at the Crucian Puddle. My belief in its eel potential had finally fired even Don's scepticism and we had taken several looks at the tiny water. It was not inspiring, little more than a rather large bowl of oxtail soup. It had been dug as a marl pit, and though there was plenty of the stuff in the ground, the farm to which it belonged had failed during the bleak days of the 1820s and the pit was left unfinished. Over a century and a half later the little marl pit was still much abused and collected all the village rubbish—prams, old bicycles and even a traffic cone all decorated the shallow end. The present farmer finally decided that enough was enough and roped off the entire pond, only allowing the village boys and a few friends to fish it. Quite how the pool had received its stock of crucians nobody remembers, but now it teems with them. There are a few roach present but these are thin, anaemic things that obviously find themselves muscled aside at feeding times by the bullish little carp. Eels have been caught there, and odd perch, but it is the crucians that are the attraction of the water, especially as occasional big ones come out every season or so.

The fascinating fact is that though the little pit teems with fish they are not easy to catch. Heavy angling pressure has made them cunning and despite their numbers they only feed for limited, frenzied periods. The bright, hot days of summer can see the water quite dead. At dusk and dawn the crucians sometimes appear ravenous and the water fizzes with bubbles as they root feverishly on the bed. Even so, they remain difficult and at times even impossible to catch. This is more than simple wariness alone; a large part of it is the idiosyncratic way in which the species feeds. Typically, the crucian will suck in and blow out an item of food several times to soften it before chewing. This behaviour makes bite indication a nightmare and any attempt at a strike nearly impossible. The bait is either out of the mouth or lightly between the lips, and the abortive strike will merely spook the fish and probably the shoal with it. No matter how small, any crucian from the Puddle is something of an achievement.

(opposite above) *A perfect crucian carp nestles on a bed of cereal. Though a small fish, it could still be one of great age and its wariness can be very frustrating*

(opposite below) *A perfectly conditioned crucian carp lies on some lilypads. The mouth of the crucian carp has no barbels about it and this may well explain their more finicky feeding behaviour than their larger carp cousins. Typically, a crucian pecks and browses rather than burrowing deep into the bottom silt. Their body is not built for long powerful runs but more for short stabbing dives, so typical of a crucian on the end of the line*

Thus it was that on 16 June the farmer arranged a small and friendly fishing match at the Puddle to celebrate the start of the new fishing season. Taking part were himself and his son, the keeper, the dairyman, Don and myself. We were each to put in £5 and the plan was for the winner to take £10 and the rest to be spent in The Swallows after the 9.30pm finish. So we gathered on 16 June at 7pm and all settled ourselves in the single swim. Large though this was, our floats were still only two or three yards apart from each other and it must be admitted that a good part of the evening was spent undoing tangles, for the farmer's casting in particular was rusty in the extreme. In fact after a while his son took over his father's casting altogether, and thus some sort of order was restored for the rest of the match. Around 7.01pm a barrage of bread, maggots and sweetcorn hit the little water and soon strings of bubbles began to lace the surface; the eager, golden, tubby crucians were obviously rummaging pop-eyed amongst this unexpected food bonanza. Sadly, however, the excitement was not shared above the water line. Six floats dipped, swayed, rose, sank—and yet not a bite was hit. Big hooks, little hooks, early strikes, late strikes, strikes hard and soft; baits massive and minute—still the floats weaved and shimmied, but not a fish was landed.

When the 8.00pm bell chimed, every single cast from each one of us had produced a bite, yet not a single bite had managed to produce a fish. Tempers seesawed. By 8.30pm we were all fishing like robots, baiting our hooks, casting (apart from the farmer), striking and trying repeatedly all over again. The conversation took different turns—rainfall, the curse of rabbits, the merits of different tractor types and the charms of the new barmaid at The Swallows were all discussed in detail, and it was almost as though there wasn't a fish in the place.

A little before 9.00pm, on a whim, I squeezed on to a size 16 hook a pinch of the hemp-based groundbait and moved the float six inches closer to the hook. Quite why a piece of groundbait dangling in mid-water should prove attractive I did not know, but at nine o'clock on the bell I felt a definite tug-tug, and swung in a 4oz crucian carp. 'Lucky sod!' 'Bet he didn't know it was on.' But I could afford to be smug, especially as I landed six similar fish within the next fifteen minutes.

At 9.20pm the farmer's son was all for calling it time, but, 'No!' said the keeper. 'Rules are rules, and there be only another ten minutes anyhow.' It was as well that he insisted, for two surprising things happened as the night began to fade.

Before the dairyman knew it, his float had gone, the line had gone tight and the rod was almost pulled from the branch rod-rest. On picking the old cane affair up, it was almost torn from his grasp and the reel screeched rustily as a giant fish bored the length of the pool. Now the dairyman didn't know much about fish like this, and his tackle and frayed line were no more up to it than he was. At the far end of the pool the fish swerved to avoid a wheelbarrow and headed back towards us, still totally in command. Virtually at our feet it buried itself into the bulrushes.

Everything went sickeningly solid and the keeper, who had thighboots on, waded out to see what could be done. He poked around and sadly informed us that the monster fish had gone. From start to finish, the fight had stretched

25 yards in a single minute. The dairyman sat with trembling fingers trying to tie on another hook and eat a pork pie at the same time.

The keeper sat down again on his box and decided to recast before the final whistle. He picked up his rod and it hooped over to an immovable weight. 'For sure,' he thought, 'I've caught the bottom.' And then it kicked. At 9.29pm precisely (I was checking to the very second) the keeper landed a crucian carp: Don put it on the scales and pronounced a weight of 2lb 10oz. The keeper had won the match by nine clear ounces. He was so happy with it, and the fish really did look so spendidly golden and round that he kicked his winnings into the drinks fund. By 9.50pm the crucian team was in The Swallows and a very serious session was underway; and Don and I talked long and hard about that lost fish of the dairyman.

———— *Crucian Carp, The Perfect Puzzle* ————

It was October half-term week in 1968. Our two floats dipped and rose on the Crucian Puddle and by mid-morning twenty-five little carp were in two buckets over our handlebars and were being cranked off to Lily Lake. I think we realised even then that Lily Lake was never going to produce for us the twenty-pounders that the keeper there claimed to see all the time, but nonetheless we got the crucians into a net and assembled the pike gear. Soon the bungs were bobbing red on the blue and gold water and the inevitable procession of jacks began to come to the gaff. After the fourth fish, I went to pull out the net for a new bait and found that the bottom had been ripped out and twenty-one crucians had made off into the depths of the lake.

'So the rumours of big crucians could well be true. We *do* know they could be in there, so let's give it a go!' Don urged. Lily Lake had changed since that October day in 1968, but not by much—the reeds had encroached a few yards, the lilies had spread, and the boathouse was simply a charred ruin. Except maybe those crucians from long ago had survived and grown as large as the valley rumours suggested.

As in the past, Don and I decided on a joint campaign for the assault at Lily Lake. We were confident that if the beauties were there, we would have them: after all, we knew all the crucian tricks. Crucians are difficult and shy it is true, but there is a well defined formula for success:

1. You fish from very first light, through dawn to eight or nine in the morning. This appears to be critical, these hours seem far better than other times of day.

2. You are very careful with your groundbaiting and lay great emphasis on a hemp-flavoured base and the most delectable of particle additives—the freshest casters, the pinkest little worms, the tastiest pinches of bread flake.

3. You employ the finest, most delicately balanced tackle with a float slotted to a pinprick and the whole set up as light and tight as possible.

4. You choose a swim hard to a tree, or weed cover, where the light remains as low as possible for as long as possible. The crucians obviously shun the sunlight with vampire-like intensity. Depth in a swim is also therefore a bonus if not an essential.

5. When bites are especially hard, it is time to try a pinch of groundbait on the hook or to set the float lower and fish the bait two inches from the bottom.

These tried and tested guidelines would catch any crucians that might still inhabit Lily Lake—or so we believed.

The deep, sheltered water was all down by the shell of the boathouse, along the dam where the lilies grew—obligingly—the thickest. There could be little doubt that the crucians, if any remained, would be in this part of the lake, and two or three sessions at most would surely be enough to prove the tales one way or another. In short, we fished together three lovely dawns, saw waterfowl glow in the sunrise, big olive tench roll over our nets with pleasing frequency, and not a single crucian. This didn't matter. They were not wholly expected, and we could fish close enough to talk the early hours away. Our words had hardly changed over the years, only perhaps become a little more serious; and so the crucianless hours went easily enough.

Two weeks passed. 'Just look at that. Can you believe it?' Don threw down a very poor quality photograph onto my desk; the fish, though, was unmistakably a crucian. It had no barbules and it was as round as a barrel and as gold as butter. And the distance was the quite unmistakable shell of the burned-out boathouse. I looked up, amazed. 'Andy caught it—yes, Andy! I've just seen him in The Swallows. He had it a fortnight ago—the very day after we'd given up, in fact. The very next morning!'

The lily lake nestles under the sunshine. This is a fabulously rich water, partly because of the run-off from the surrounding agricultural lands. An estate lake like this is typically a sink and collects a great deal of nitrate. One effect of this is increased weed growth and encouraging food stocks

On estate lakes the deepest water will typically be found by the dam. In winter this is generally the area to choose, but it is not always the case in the summer months

A large crucian carp is held to the early morning light

A lovely shot of one of England's favourite fish—the tench. It is interesting that in the valley a big tench (by national standards) is very rare. The large tench today seem to be very much a species of the huge gravel-pit complex. Perhaps the estate lake environment is a little too tired and parasite-ridden to produce the biggest of the species. Or perhaps tench spawn in these shallow, warm, weedy environments too prolifically. Populations then rise, competition for food becomes intense, and the average size of fish declines. Another factor in the decline of individual big fish must be the stocking of mirror carp which again hoover up valuable tench food in vast quantities

5am and Don settled back into the deep dark swim into the boathouse. I began to unpack, and then was stopped short by that little voice of instinct that speaks to each of us at some time. Suddenly I decided to walk the whole lake rather than fish immediately, and an hour later was down at the far end where the water was shallow, clear and weed-free. The sun was already up, burning on the surface and every grain of sand was quite visible. Six yards from me a very large, very beautiful crucian carp rolled with a slow deliberation. As it disappeared from the light, so it disappeared into crystal water. It just could not be seen. By 6.20am four crucians had appeared from invisibility—or the one crucian had rolled four times. Whichever it was, I had seen quite enough.

A very beautiful female tench lies in the landing net, and the float that spelt her downfall hangs from the rim

That day we caught two crucians and the next, four. The swim was eighteen inches deep, we only caught when it was flooded with light, and the bites pulled the rod-tip round and made the reel handle spin. Nor did it seem to matter how heavy the tackle was but a crucian would hang itself sooner rather than later. Of course, how long they would have gone on like this is doubtful; but it just proves that a sure knowledge of crucians is always a suspect thing.

The Puddle Express

The sun was close to setting. The daytime breeze had died away and Don's float lay hard against the reeds of the Puddle, damselflies and hordes of tiny crucians flipping around it. These crucians had made maggot an impossibility, and even flake was whittled to nothing. Two grains of corn proved more difficult and three grains lasted for a good ten minutes. Then as night approached the shadows lay themselves down in a period of comparative peace.

Don's float sat up, moved fast to the north and disappeared. The line shot tight and the Puddle express pistolled up the pond, back again into the reeds and away, free as a bird, before Don, in truth, had done a thing. It might have been a humiliating experience, yet the creature had been quite beyond control largely because of its remarkable speed—that, and the Puddle's extremely tight space, together made any conventional stab at playing out of the question. It was all quite dizzying and Don packed up and drove to my cottage.

'It couldn't have been a particularly huge fish,' he said, 'or there would have been a bow wave. Remember the water's only two or three feet deep at the most. I felt it had the power of a tench, but somehow it moved too quickly—it was faster off the mark than a tench ever is. It was certainly a fish that knew where it was going and had absolutely no hesitation. I feel really it has to be a wild carp that has got in there. I'm going back, though. We'd all like to be sure.' I guess he had some three hours sleep in an armchair and then I heard him moving around before dawn. The front door clicked shut and his car nosed out once more into the night.

Again his float was cast to the reeds, but this time Don sat on the south side of the pond rather than the east so that he could pull the fish out of the reeds after that first lightning lap of the Puddle. Also, he doubled the line strength to 8lb breaking strain. A size 8 hook replaced the 14 and he began with three pieces of corn.

His plan was to bait very heavily with hemp, maggots, mashed bread and corn: he wanted to create a bit of havoc at the Puddle that morning and lull the monster's caution after the previous night's scare. At dawn, the crucians would be most likely to feed their hardest and the mayhem should spread around the pond and get everything well on the boil.

By daylight, the crucians were responding madly to the ploy and the swim, which was really half the entire Puddle, was going berserk. Jumping, rolling, bubbling crucians were everywhere and the three grains of corn were constantly nibbled and torn from the hook by the greedy sucking little lips. Don deeply regretted not bringing any other type of bait but bread, and so he stepped up the three grains one by one until eventually ten grains were crammed from point to eye, and even a little way up the line. They presented

Hanging on!

The Puddle express nears the net

This shot rather explains the success of the chub in the Crucian Puddle. The mouth of the fish dwarfs a size 4 hook and is obviously quite capable of engulfing a two- or even a four-ounce crucian carp. Food can never have been more plentiful or more nutritious for the newly transported fish; and, what is more, he had it all to himself!

an unholy gobful lying there on the Puddle bed, but still, Don reckoned, they would have the element of surprise.

It was a bold plan, but an unsuccessful one that morning. Perhaps the danger of corn after the previous night's near escape warned the monster off. Perhaps the glob of corn looked totally unbelievable to a fish that had presumably acquired not a little wisdom. Perhaps the tackle was too obviously heavy in a rapidly lightening, shallow and virtually weedless pond. The direct way had not proved the right one.

Evening, and Don was back. He was going to follow the same plan and try to get the crucians back on the feed in earnest. He felt it was essential to get the puddle vibrating and to stir whatever it was into a feeding mode. The tackle though, was scaled down to a mid-point with 5lb line; for baits he had taken an array of nibble-proof worms, peanuts and hard-skinned luncheon meat.

The evening passed balmy and pleasant, with many flicks on the line and one very sharp lift of a foot or more, probably a line bite from a good fish, perhaps even the monster. On the point of darkness there was a large swirl and several crucians scattered. A predator or a bigger fish simply moving through, causing panic? However, the upheaval had convinced Don that the monster was in the swim and was active: he put a large lump of meat on a size 4 hook and swung it out close to the reeds. The oil from the bait made circles in the gloomy water, and the line hung limp. Don, tense and alert, had left the hook proud of the meat and was prepared for a very quick strike to keep the fish from the rushes on that first mad run. Half-an-hour passed, and then the line moved away. There was nothing dramatic about it, just the steady, positive sweep of a very decided fish.

The fight followed all the rules of past ones. The fish moved scorching fast and was bold and determined, but this time all the pressure could be heaped on direct to keep the fish from the reeds. It huffed and it puffed but it could not flatten the rushes down, and yard by yard the 'whatever' was pulled across the Puddle. The torch beam shone on large brassy scales and a long body. Yes, a wildie. It was a good one, though. Don guessed 6lb.

The net bent to the weight and Don struggled into the field with his prize. A stoat scampered off in front of him. He had bent to the very mouth of the fish before he saw what it was and exclaimed in surprise. This was no wildie, though it did weigh around the 6lb mark as he had guessed.

Quite how a chub had got into the isolated pond we had no explanation. Guesswork suggested an escaped bait, meant perhaps for an eel. What *was* evident was the condition of the fish: the Puddle possessed the means not only to sustain it but to allow it to thrive. Obviously those crucians swirled with real purpose: this great chub was their harvester and on them had grown fat as an ox and as gold as butter. The Puddle monster was at last exposed.

—————— *A Forgotten Bream Shoal* ——————

On the fringes of the valley lies a famous lake known by several aliases invented by those wishing to shield its identity. Here we will call the five acres of shallow water 'the bream lake,' although for those few men fortunate enough to fish here, the major and compelling attraction is the stock of mirror carp. The bream, huge as they are, have by and large lived in the shadow of their larger cousins and been ignored. In fact, those few bream landed have generally been taken by carp anglers and perhaps have not been appreciated as much as their size and beauty deserve.

As far as I can tell, the water was created around a hundred years ago and because of its comparatively recent date, silting is still at a minimum. The shallowness that has overtaken the water is due more now to lack of spring water and shrinkage from the top, rather than from the bottom! In recent years abstraction for the surrounding potato lands has drained water away from the lake, and the stanchions of the boathouse tell a sad story: for decades the water washed against the great wooden pillars that hold the elaborate structure out over the lake and obviously a tide-mark was produced— a tide-mark that now stands at almost two feet above the present water-line. It is hard to imagine the amount of rain and winter snow needed to replenish the depleted springs and restore the bream lake to its former height and glory.

The falling levels had threatened the water way back in 1976 when a huge population of bream and roach appeared to be in distress. That year, very large fish of both species as well as a few sizeable carp were found dead in June. In

A classic shot of the bream lake in the olden days. It is hard to know whether to gasp at the fabulous shape of the cradled mirror carp or at the marvellously ornate boat-house behind it. On the extreme right of the picture are those great pillars that support the structure and are bedded into the lake

all probability the stress of spawning and the low oxygen levels combined to kill these fish off, and the decision was made to net as many survivors as possible and to take them to safer havens. The lack of depth, and the absence of snags and deep channels allowed a very successful operation to take place, and thousands of fish were transported to other waters, generally outside the valley and even out of the county. In the aftermath of all this, the bream lake was generally forgotten by most local anglers.

Indeed, it was not until a decade after that netting that I thought it worthwhile to visit the place. How very glad I've always been that I did! As I said to Don, enthusing about its undiminished beauty,

'You remember how murky the bream lake used to be, a real pea-souper? Well, all that colour was gone, and it had become crystal clear, really gin-like stuff. You could see every pebble . . . and for a while I didn't see a fish. I looked everywhere and apart from occasional eels there didn't seem to be a thing. It was one of the most remarkable occasions I've experienced, of being over big carp and, as it turned out, big bream, and not having a single clue for ages. How fish can do this is a mystery to me—camouflage just doesn't come into it. It's rather as though in certain lights and water clarities fish can become all but invisible, and in fact if it weren't for the sun shining directly on them and giving them a shadow, you'd never spot them at all. I was on the point of writing the lake off, I'd walked round it *twice* and only then saw them almost by chance.

'I suppose the rest is history, since this is the water so many of my big carp came from; but there were big bream, too, so if it's big bream you fancy now, give it a look yourself. My experiences seem to suggest that there is one shoal of large fish left, and that includes individuals between 8lb and possibly 11lb or 12lb. They're real crackers. I landed a "nine" a couple of years back and it was built like a barn. What I guess happened was that after the netting, so few fish remained that they could never get a hold again. The changing character of the water itself helped to see to that. Remember how the place used to heave with bream, from skimmers to real slabs? Well, that number of fish kept the water permanently cloudy, apart from in really cold weather—so without this mass of fish the lake went clear very quickly, and in clear water what fry and fingerlings were produced—quite a small number now—could be hunted easily by eels, kingfishers, grebes, cormorants—you name the number of predators that a big lake near the coast is going to attract. So there was a smaller number of parent fish, a smaller number of fry produced, and more successful predation, and the consequent decline in numbers was pretty well guaranteed.

'What we've got now is a real specimen lake, but there are only thirteen or fourteen fish and when they go, there will be nothing left to follow behind them. The carp themselves are hardly more numerous and I doubt whether there are more than eighteen of them. So really there are probably less than forty fish, barring eels, in the entire lake. What's more, catching the bream isn't easy—I've tried, and failed! The few that I've caught came in a chance fashion when I had put out bait for the carp and was sitting on it, and then I got the odd bite. Hardly any big deal, eh? But the interesting thing is, that even on carp tackle those bream still manage to fight a bit! But I'm sure there are nicer ways of catching them, and there are ways of going for the bream specifically. On

There can be no sadder sight than the removal of a large fish, dead before its time. This large bream had died in mid-June when water temperatures have rocketed, oxygen levels have fallen and the fish has not been able to recover from the stress of spawning

The big bream that remain are clearly visible moving in the crystal water

your side is the fact that they are always very visible, and I rather fancy long-distance stalking for winkling a couple out. Still, it's your decision. There they are . . .'

Don arrived at the bream lake during a lull in the hot weather towards the end of September, and for a very long while just sat looking over the water. It was every bit as beautiful as he remembered it, even under a thick mantle of cloud. It was a very still day; the rain of the morning had ceased and now the water was reflecting every leaf of the bankside trees, so it was a while before any fish could be seen even in the very low water. Still, Don had the sense not to move and had found a good vantage point, and gradually succeeded in making out the carp, those lovely fish for which the lake has become increasingly famous.

A large group of them had settled right in front of him, and for an hour threw up occasional bubbles, the odd fish tipping to investigate the bed. By and large though, these big carp were just drifting, dorsals stretching as they enjoyed the clammy conditions and the warm, close air. One extremely pale mirror stayed very still almost at his feet for twenty minutes—it was quite awake, with its eyes rolling and its fins holding its body steady; Don put out a worm to settle a foot from its head, and it never moved. Then he flicked in half-a-dozen grains of corn and the fish turned itself slightly to watch them fall; its fins worked more anxiously now, and then very slowly it moved away to deeper water. Don watched it trundle out towards the island, and realised that a big carp is its own master and will not be hurried by anyone.

This little episode did, however, work out well in the end. As Don followed the big fish through binoculars it was quite possible to distinguish not only its sparsely scaled back, but also several smaller shapes around it. That is, they might have been smaller, but not by a great deal: these were the bream, milling around and about the great plateau of sand.

Two obvious plans sprang to Don's mind. The first was to groundbait neatly

The rain absolutely pelts down upon both man and fish. But who cares?

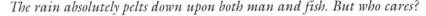

and tightly and carefully, and hemp seed, hemp-based cereal, casters and little red worms had been brought for the purpose. The initial splash of twenty small balls, even with a minute between them, would disturb the shoal to some degree, but it would probably reappear and perhaps begin to feed. A nicely presented cocktail of caster and worm, or even a lump of flake had every chance of success.

The second approach was the one that Don really favoured and in fact tried first. A 12ft rod, 4lb line, bomb, long 3lb link, size 16 hook and two red worms sailed out to land in amongst the fish.

There followed an excruciating period. Over and over the bream nosed past his bait. From a distance it was very difficult to see whether they actually saw it or not, but in such clear water at such close range, Don guessed that several fish must have been quite aware of the worms twitching on the bottom. Why would they not feed? Was the tackle obvious to them? Were the worms simply unattractive?

He reeled them in and tried one larger lobworm, injected with air so that it floated some six or seven inches above the sand plateau. Again the bream moved round to investigate, but again, not one fish made anything like a serious attempt on it. A piece of flake was ignored and so was a bunch of casters. Or not quite: a 1lb eel came wriggling and protesting to the bank.

At this point Don found it impossible to resist the challenge of the carp, still moving comparatively fearlessly in his area of the lake; but although he tried floaters and every type of bottom bait, his indicators remained motionless and the carp proved every bit as hard to tempt as the bream. Already the sun was beginning to set and he decided that finally some other tactic would have to be employed: so the initial groundbaiting plan was called into operation.

About fifty yards from the bream down towards the old boathouse, the plateau shelves slightly into a large, twenty-yard-radius saucer. Into this, Don piled twenty to twenty-five balls of high-intensity, hemp-based caster-filled groundbait. The noise of entry did disturb one smaller carp in the area but the bream remained quite unalarmed. As the sun disappeared and the early evening came on, Don cast two rods out into the saucer, one baited with casters and the second with worm. Hiding himself behind the trunk of one of the great copper beech trees, he set himself to wait as long as the bream might demand of him.

Thanks to the cloud it was a warm night, and although he had not come prepared for a long session he did not get cold. Hunger was assuaged by some bread and sweetcorn, and as for his thirst, well, he tried not to think of the boys down at The Swallows! The night continued very calm indeed without a ripple on the water. On two occasions large carp exploded from the stillness and the ripples that they caused lapped gently at his feet. A badger wandered past him, ten yards back in the undergrowth, grunting and shuffling through the fallen leaves and dead branches. A fox barked once and pheasants chorused from the trees around. He lost himself in thought and in the warm beauty of the night, and the fact that his indicators never moved a millimetre was of little matter.

He remembered the Hall clock striking three and nothing else, so probably fell asleep. He was awoken by a chill wind that had developed around dawn, a nasty, snappy little breeze coming right down the lake from the north and rolling in wisps of mist. Now there was a good chop on the lake and the trees all round were swaying and whispering to each other. Intuitively Don sensed his chance, and reeled in the baits to replace them. He was not too pleased to find the casters sucked on the one hook and the worm all but taken from the other—probably the culprits were small eels, but this evidence of fish interest sent a quiver of anticipation through him. Within two minutes fresh bait were out there in the saucer and the bobbins were reset. Two hours later the right-hand bobbin moved towards the butt.

Don knew well to let the bite develop, and he waited till the reel handle was moving slowly round and round before bending down, picking the rod up and striking deliberately over his right shoulder. That was it. He knew immediately that this was neither eel nor carp. The fight was not spectacular but it was long and solid, and knowing exactly what was on the end, at times quite heart-stopping. The bream itself was so deep that three times it grounded in the very shallow water close into the bank, and each time Don had to pile the pressure on to keep it moving. At the last the big fish tired and lay on its side, and Don could skate it over the water that was only 4in in depth. A net was not necessary and Don simply beached it on the soft wet sand. He unhooked it and then waded in until there was depth enough to let it swim away freely. He had had one bream. That was enough. He packed and left, wondering how many seasons the lake and its precious population of big fish would continue to survive.

The bream in profile showing its large extendable lips, so adept at hoovering up food from the lake bed. In some ways bream are very greedy and yet in others they remain the most delicate of feeders, quite able to detect heavy line or a large hook. It is rare for a large bait to be engulfed at once and generally the bream will simply hold it between its lips and perhaps move off taking it very slowly into the mouth. If it then feels any resistance during this action the bait is immediately rejected

The Year Ends

— Old Money Used Up —

On the fringe of the valley a large old farm stands situated on gravel and sand, land which traditionally was hard work and good only for shooting. It was this that attracted the family during the last century to the place, and surprisingly, this old money lasted over two wars and several depressions. It was only rocketing inflation in the 1970s that made the first serious incursions upon it, and in the end, succour came from an unexpected source. The nearest town was to be bypassed, and hoggin and gravel were needed by the mountainful: by being plundered of its minerals, the arid estate was saved. The chain of craters so near the river's headwaters were soon cool green lakes, and as protected bird sanctuaries, rumour had it that the fishing potential of the waters was something special—indeed, I was once shown a photograph of a quite mammoth roach, reputed to be over 3lb. The fish must have been all of that, and it came from a water the size of an average sitting-room: to explain, that particular water was the duck-breeding pen, situated so close to the river that when it flooded, roach and dace could enter and grow huge on the lavish,

Sunrise at the new pit. When first fishing a pike water it is wise to go for sessions that last from before dawn till after darkness. Pit pike seem to have their own fairly limited feeding spells and these can take place at any time in the day. The only way of discovering them is to be actually there, fishing

high-protein duck food. Apparently dace the size of chub, and roach like bream tussled with King Eiders for the pellets.

Less bizarre, but equally exciting, was said to be the largest, oldest, and deepest of the pits; it had a sublime turquoise colour to it, and for sure again held roach and dace from the river, and also pike. These in particular were said to be enormous, and as far as the owner was concerned, they were the terror of the wildfowl—nothing less than an albatross was safe. When in desperation he phoned us, I was happy to offer our pike removal services lest the mallard follow the same fate!

Even in autumn, the water smiled like summer. The Canadian pondweed was rich and the colour was the see-through blue of an Adriatic sky. As the sun rose, it was possible to see dace shoals following the contours. They were superb fish, and when a roach rolled all I could do was gasp. The early years of a new water are so dynamic that you just have to be there to appreciate it. Growth rates of all fish species are exceptionally rapid in the first ten to fifteen years of a new pit's life. Perhaps this has something to do with the minerals released into the water, or perhaps it is because the food supplies are fresh, ungrazed and therefore very rich. Frequently too fish stocks are low and so competition is at a minimum, and what fish do exist can rocket forward. At these periods, in these places, the piking potential is enormous.

'And remember, I don't want them put in the river, they'll be back in with the first flood eating my ducks. If you won't kill them, take them away, *miles* away!' On an unknown water we would have been stupid to take any chances with tackle. Twelve-foot rods, 12lb line, new traces, the strongest hooks and knots tried and tested made up the gear. A couple of the rods were set up to float paternoster baits close to snags, and a further two were equipped with drifter floats so we could capitalise on the slight breeze and explore as much of the water as possible. With no prior knowledge of the water it was vital to keep exploring until fish were contacted.

We moved steadily round the pit and on the stroke of one, Don's float moved purposefully away. This fish was a beautifully marked, nicely proportioned 12lb hen. Whoever thinks pike an ugly species had not seen this fish, tummy like snow, her spots on fire. Into a sack she went, and soon a whole string of them followed, seven pike in two hours, all between 10 and 15lb, all beautiful and all unmarked.

The owner of this waterland was unimpressed: 'I bet there are ducks in them now. Should we open one up to see?' The look on our faces discouraged surgery, and the Land-Rover drove away with a breezy pip of the horn.

Around three the float went again; the rod stayed round and would not come up. This was it: a wondrous, pristine, glowing mid-twenty. 'A photograph Don, I think!' As I held the fish at the water's edge, the owner reappeared and cursed it. The pike squirmed. I 'slipped' . . . then it was free and dropped into three feet of water. 'Get it! Get the damn thing quick! Grab its tail!' I waded as clumsily as I could, making purposefully feeble stabs at its flank. It bolted from sight. 'Oh, hell. Make damn sure you don't drop away more of the rotten things.'

Finally we had loaded a hundredweight of fine pike into tanks and sloshed our way off down the lane from the farm. Half-a-mile through the gates I

(above left) *A good (if rather thin) double is held in front of the pale, winter light*

(above right) *A wonderful example of a pike, spotted like a leopard and built like a tank. To kill a pike like this is a travesty. It is a valuable predator in any type of fishery, not only killing weak and wounded fish but also culling the number of destructive jack pike that its own eggs produce annually*

stopped and switched off the engine, and we sat in the lane. Where on earth could we put these wonderful pike where the eel-netter wouldn't find them, where they wouldn't upset the finely tuned balance of Nature, where there would be enough fish to sustain their chunky frames? Try as we might we could think of nowhere.

There was only one thing to do, and we waited.

It was five hours before the lights in the big house were all switched off, and we knew the farmer was away to bed.

And then . . !

Later that evening it was obvious that Don's depression had not been

*The beauty of the big unmarked
pike against the winter bank*

A fish to be returned

relieved either by the meeting with the eel-netter or by the capture of a good pike. He had appeared restless since the end of the summer—obviously the valley for him was no more than a staging-post, and an interlude, and now he needed more physically and mentally demanding challenges. He had long been questioning me about my own adventures after ferox trout in the Highlands and mahseer in Asia, and it was evident that he still had the money and the desire to travel. He told me he would soon be on his way again.

And a few days later he was gone.

The Buddha: Closing In

Soon after Don's departure, autumn gave way to winter in a matter of days. A period of near ceaseless rain followed: rain, and a cold that chilled the heart. The Gardener's Lake was now desolate. The weed died off the surface in days, and the trees stood gaunt and bare; though water remained clear, clearer now the daphnia clouds had succumbed to the cold. For a while I was apprehensive and feared that the sudden dip in temperatures could have ruined my chances on the water for this season at least. I was worried that the Buddha might have settled quickly into a winter torpor somewhere in the deep water by the dam, shrouded in dead weed and fallen leaves. My anxieties were unfounded, however. On a still, comparatively mild day, several of the fish could be seen, pale and ghostlike in the gloom, cruising ceaselessly through the thin water. The summer harvest had now gone, but the fish needed to continue feeding heavily to build up a certain amount of reserve for the winter. Now they were really having to work for their food, and this realisation gave me hope that all chance of the Buddha had not vanished. Actually, the more I watched the fish that afternoon, the more I realised how much my chances were all at once improving. Assuming the Buddha to be as wakeful as his lesser companions, he would be deprived by the cold of all his familiar food and would be all the more likely to investigate an alien source. If enough food could be introduced day by day to keep the carp interested and on the feed, the Buddha must, surely, soon move on to the bait and become vulnerable. At dusk, one good fish swimming higher than its companions began to take odd offerings from the surface. Some crust disappeared, a few biscuits, and also a floating red boilie I happened by pure chance to have with me. It was the boilie that persuaded me to bait the lake quite heavily with the modern high-protein bait. Quite why I had tended to fight shy of them in the past I cannot totally define; in part, maybe, they and the methods they are used with seem to be an unwelcome intrusion into waters that are still relatively naive and it seemed unnecessary to me to go quite so far up the ladder of angling technique. And, I also suspected that estate lakes do not respond as well to larger baits as to particles, in the summer especially when there is so much natural food available. In the winter, of course, food supplies were less and larger, conventional baits more acceptable to hungry carp, and I was desperate enough to try anything for this fish.

Autumn moves on apace and the leaves begin to dust the surface of the Gardener's Lake. This is always a difficult part of the fishing year as water temperatures begin to tumble and leaves themselves sour the water to a great extent

In went the boilies, each day. I lost some at first: the summer brood of four coots had all survived and the pond in the cold was a cramped place for six grown birds. Squabbles were constant, and I realised on the third day that the boilies had not gone unnoticed by the beady black eyes. I began to introduce them in the deepest area on the fringe of the alders and to sit guard a while until the dim-witted little birds had forgotten what they were looking for.

Though the weather continued to deteriorate, my hopes remained high and after a week I began to fish. I doubt if I could have fished harder, longer or better. I took great care to ensure the tackle was flawless and that every knot and swivel on the 11lb line was tested and retested. I still refused to use a hair rig, and side-hooked a sweet-flavoured boilie that was made buoyant with polystyrene to counteract the weight of the size 6 it was attached to. My approach was Apache-like and for seventy-two miserable, sleet-filled hours, I only left the lake in short bursts. However, the only run came in the second day and resulted in a briefly hooked male coot that was very cross with those round him for the rest of the twilight.

On the third day I returned in the dark hours before dawn, but that day proved no better than the previous two and I was glad to pack away after a very dreary session. Around 3pm, however, I had noticed a very large 'flat' smooth a sizeable area of wind lane. I watched the area like a hawk for minutes

The inside of a keeper's shed from centuries past. There is every tool here for the destruction of vermin . . . and the unwary poacher

thereafter: no bird resurfaced anywhere in the vicinity and I could only conclude that the disturbance was created by fin rather than by feather. Anyway, it decided me to return on the fourth day.

There was a bleak sunshine that gave no warmth but just a little more visibility into the dark water; although this was to no advantage, as the lake seemed to be quite without life. After an hour, I settled under the thickest of the alders to eat some breakfast and watch quietly. With the help of Polaroid glasses a quite large area of polished, clear gravel about seven feet from the bank could be seen; it contrasted vividly with the surrounding detritus of fallen leaf and moribund weed and I could only think that it marked the mouth of a spring or that it was a carp's tabletop.

In the mid-afternoon I had my answer. A small carp detached itself from the gloom and swam across the gravel. Its dark form was startlingly visible but it did not stop long. It upped and was on its way and its place was taken by the unmistakably huge, ponderous shape of the Buddha.

For several minutes the giant fish hovered over the gravel window at my feet, occasionally tipping to investigate items on the bed. When at last it melted into the darkness beneath the alder trunk, I moved, sliding away from my rod. The light was beginning to go. My eyes could barely trace the two grains of corn on a size 6 hook onto the now dull flash of white. Eight or ten loose grains

The dream—a great fish landed at last　　　　　(opposite) *The owl watches the game*

followed and I lay back amongst wet leaves watching the float just a stick's length out from me.

Even as the day ebbed, my confidence grew. It seemed so fitting that the Buddha and I should come together right at the end in this way, and I felt sure that I was meant to catch the great carp that night. More prosaically, the Buddha must have had his guard very low in the gathering dark, tight undercover over his now favourite feeding ground. If ever I had the chance of the Buddha, it had to be now.

The time of waiting was in fact quite short—forty minutes, I guess—but it seemed endless as I reviewed the year almost gone; though I could no longer face the future with the boundless optimism of a youngster, at least I could see years of promise and plenty left in the valley. All I needed now was this final superb fish.

But still I waited . . . until the Buddha decided it was time.

The float went under and the rod tip whizzed around: I was on my feet, hauling to the left, straining to keep the fish from the alder. I sank to my knees, thighs, beyond, in silt, striving to get a better angle. I made it. The carp gave up and heaved around to its left, away from me, out into open water.

I let him pull off ten yards of line and allowed him to play around out there

A success that will have to wait for another year

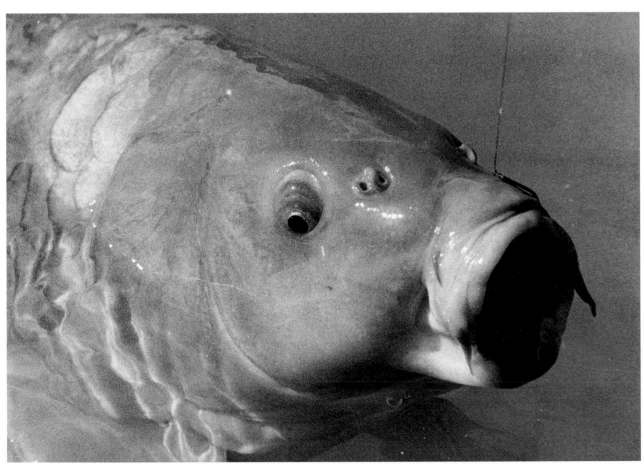

in the deep, snag-free central channel. He plugged here and there and I was content to let him tire slowly. I could wait all night if he demanded it, if he had that much in him. An occasional thump of the rod tip worried me and though his runs were powerful still, they were short and easily containable. Continue like this, I felt, and I had no worries.

I did wrong. In fact I had let him regroup his forces out there, cruising in the darkness, and when he decided his strength was returned, he doubled back in a charge for the alder roots, travelling far faster than I could reel. With a couple of yards of slack to the good, he made sanctuary. Believe me, I saw the tree shudder against the sky as he forced into it and lay safe in the stronghold branches.

I pulled: everything was solid. I handlined: solid. I let off slack. Half-an-hour passed, and the cold in my body was intense: still solid. I stumbled in to my waist, chest and then shoulders and followed the line down into the dark, bitterly cold water.

The hook was buried past the barb into the alder root.

I sat at the Hall and they laughed and tried to console me. Sportsmen themselves, they understood and gave me measured, sound sympathy, but not too much. Several whiskies restored the final parts of my sanity and logic and at last I saw that there are greater disasters in life than letting a hooked fish swim free. And even if he had won the fight, I had tricked him at the end. What a summer, and what a climax it had all been!

———————— *Squaring The Circle* ————————

As the shortest day approached and as my year with the Buddha was done, I turned to the tidal river and the question of Don's roach. For several reasons, my attention turned to the one bend half way down the stretch. I figured that any roach in the area would make for its depth and for the fact that it was heavily reeded along the margins. I felt this would give protection to any fish from the cold and from the worst of the currents that were now quite substantial after long weeks of rain. The colour was not back in the water and I felt it would be worthwhile sitting over mashed bread around dusk. A small discomfort for possible high reward.

I had pre-baited for quite a few days. Over the years I have discovered that the taste of bread is quite addictive to roach. The fish are just as easily tamed as any living creature, and the dribble of nourishing white bread found once, will soon become an important item in the daily round.

It had been the roach angler's favourite type of day: low cloud sweeping before a wet westerly wind, and light never a pitch above gloom—it was this darkness that in fact decided me upon the session on that particular day. Days of low light levels almost invariably see roach feeding off and on through the daytime, and at dusk this activity builds to a crescendo. After such a day roach are simply bound to feed: when it is cold and clear they might feed only very late at night, as late as midnight, or not at all.

On the face of it, one fish from so long a stretch of river might have seemed

This sight of the shy water vole about to enter the water from its pipe home should not be a rare one to the roach fisherman. Complete quietness and perfect camouflage are often necessary to outwit the large roach from a small river and indeed the shy water vole itself

an impossible venture, but I knew it not to be so. In fact I was quite confident as I put in the two rod rests and threw three slices of mashed bread into the deepest part of the swim, about five feet, some two yards from the reed fringe. My only concern was that the chub would come along and spook things in his own stupid clodhopping way. Soon I was in amongst the damp, dead sedge, on my cushion, the bobbin almost at my nose, looking across the river to the brightest band of the sky in the west.

Almost from the start I knew I was not alone on the bend. Occasionally very small strings of bubbles rose here and there. There might only be four or five

(opposite) *A perfect winter roach day. The air is mild but windy and rain comes trucking in from the west. The earth is sodden and the river has a good colour to it, and the roach are bound to be on the feed*

or six each time, but they were very small and precise, the exact sort a roach pushes through his gills as he forages. The fact that invariably they surfaced above where I expected the bread to be lying only encouraged me. Twice, too, the bobbin flicked quickly, as though a bat had glanced the line with his wing; but the rod tip was under water and the only culprit could be a fish passing in the now quarter light. I knew it was only a matter of time before the bobbin would truly soar . . .

Frankly, I was surprised I had to wait till 6pm. In all probability I had thrown in a slice of bread too many; the fish were simply pecking here and there and my flake stood little chance of being taken first from amongst so many other mouthfuls of white. At 6.04pm the bobbin lifted a quick inch. Another line bite? A dropped bait? A roach with the bait in its lips, sucking, tasting, preparing to take it deep into its mouth when he would turn away and swallow it and chew? If so, there would be a pause of five or ten seconds and then the bobbin would hammer to the butt . . . In the event, the bobbin was a blur!

The fish rolled at once, heavily, by my feet so I knew it was not the chub. I kept him off balance and he was in the net within, I guess, twelve seconds. Sixteen inches long. Fabulous. Not a three, but who cared? Don's fish? I hoped so and believed it more than likely. Though roach will travel miles in a week this was the only big lone fish seen in the river and I was sure it had not been a shoal in front of me: what activity there was had suggested a single, large and busy fish. I certainly did not have the confidence to fish on, and anyway I was freezing. It was 6.30pm and the bolts on the old door would have been slid back, the beer pumps turned on and the fire lit.

'A cod for yer! Or are you too fussy for that even? I saw your car and thought we could barter: 5lb of cod for a pint isn't bad.' Nor was it, for fish fresh as the surf. We didn't talk a great deal, quite content to watch the logs in the grate, feel the warmth come creeping in.

'So, we've both been fishing then?' he said. 'It was me grandad taught me. He used to be keeper up at Frog Hall, a great tall man he was, always dressed in black—for night-work see. Who taught you then?'

'It was my grandmother.'

So our love for the valley is like the river, a love that runs on and on and is passed from one of us to the next in line. Through this love, we all hold on to our piece of immortality, and while the valley lives there will be a piece of every man that will never die.

(opposite above) *A beautiful roach, the real gentle giant of the river*

(opposite below) *A foxcub peers out from a hollow tree trunk*

INDEX

Numbers in *italics* indicate illustrations